# MOON

DUBROVNIK
& THE DALMATIAN COAST

SHANN FOUNTAIN ČULO

Contents

DUBROVNIK 8
History 9
Planning Your Time 11
Orientation 11

Sights 12
Old Town 12
  ❰ Gradske zidine 12
  ❰ Stradun 12
  Franjevački samostan 14
  ❰ War Photo Limited 14
  Žudioska 15
  Palača Sponza 15
  Crkva svetog Vlaha 15
  Orlando's Column 15
  Onofrio's Little Fountain 16
  Knežev dvor 16
  Galerija Dulčić-Masle-Pulitika 17
  Katedrala 17
  Tvrđava Sv. Ivan 17
  ❰ Pustijerna 17
  Od Puča 18
  Etnografski muzej Rupe 18
  Dominikanski samostan 18
East of the City Walls 19
  Revelin Fortress 19
  Lazareti 19
  Umjetnička Galerija 19
Off the Coast 19
  ❰ Lokrum 19
Beaches 20

Entertainment, Shopping, and Recreation 20
Entertainment and Events 20
  Nightlife 20
  Festivals and Events 21

Shopping 21
Sports and Recreation 21

Accommodations 22
Inside the City Walls 22
Outside the City Walls 22

Food 24

Information and Services ... 26
Tours and Tourist Information 26
Communication 26
Other Services 26

Getting There and Around .. 27
Getting There 27
  Air 27
  Bus 27
  Car 27
  Boat 27
Getting Around 27
  Bus 27
  Taxi 27
  Car 27
  Boat 27

Around Dubrovnik 28
  ❰ Trsteno 28
Cavtat 28
Elafiti Islands 29
  Koločep 29
  Lopud 29
  Šipan 30
  ❰ Pelješac Peninsula 30
  Orebić 30

Ston and Mali Ston 31
Wineries 32

SOUTHERN DALMATIA 33

Planning Your Time 33

Split 36

History 36

Sights 38
  ◖ Diocletian's Palace 38
  Katedrala svetog Dujma 38
  Krstionica 39
  Etnografski muzej 39
  Papalićeva Palača 40
  Porta Aurea 40
  Arheološki muzej 40
  Marjan Peninsula 40
  ◖ Galerija Ivana Meštrovića 40
  Bačvice 41
  Tvrđava Gripe 41

Entertainment and Events 41
  Nightlife 41
  Festivals and Events 41

Shopping 41

Sports and Recreation 42
  Spectator Sports 42

Accommodations 42

Food 43

Information and Services 43

Getting There and Around 44

Around Split 44

Omiš 45

Sights 45

Accommodations 45

Food 46

Information and Services 46

Getting There and Around 46
Cetina Gorge 46
Sports and Recreation 46
Food 46

Makarska Riviera 47

Brela 47
  Beaches 47
  Accommodations and Food 47
  Information and Services 47
  Getting There and Around 47

Baška Voda 48
  Accommodations and Food 48
  Information and Services 48
  Getting There and Around 48

Makarska 48
  Accommodations and Food 49
  Information and Services 49
  Getting There and Around 49

Southern Dalmatian Islands 50

Brač 50
  Supetar 50
  Bol 51
  Around Brač 52
  Wineries 52
  Getting There and Around 52

◖ Hvar 52
  Hvar Town 52
  Palmižana 56
  Stari Grad 56
  Jelsa 57
  Sveta Nedelja 57
  Svirče 57
  Vrboska 57
  Sućuraj 58
  Getting There and Around 58

◖ Vis 58
  Vis Town 58
  Komiža 60
  Stončića 61

Rukavac and Biševo 61
Wineries 61
Getting There and Around........... 62
◐ **Korčula**........................ 62
Korčula Town..................... 62
Lumbarda......................... 64
Vela Luka 64
Getting There and Around........... 65
Skoji Islands...................... 65
Lastovo 65
Festivals......................... 65
Accommodations and Food........ 66
Getting There and Around........... 66
◐ **Mljet** 66
Sights and Recreation 66
Accommodations 67
Food 67
Getting There and Around........... 67

NORTHERN DALMATIA............... 69
Planning Your Time............... 70

Zadar 72
History........................... 72
Sights............................ 72
◐ The Forum 72
Trg Opatice Čike 73
Franjevački samostan............. 73
Morske orgulje................... 74
City Walls 74
Narodni trg...................... 74
Crkva svetog Šimuna 75
Trg pet bunara................... 75
Varoš Quarter 75
Beaches.......................... 75
Entertainment and Events 75
Nightlife 75
Festivals and Events 76
Accommodations.................. 76

Food............................. 76
Information and Services......... 78
Getting There and Around........ 78

Islands Around Zadar......... 79
Ugljan........................... 79
Pašman 79
Iž................................ 79
◐ **Dugi Otok** 80
Silba 80

Paklenica National Park..... 81
Sports and Recreation 81
Hiking and Tours.................. 81
Climbing......................... 82
Accommodations.................. 82
Food............................. 83
Getting There and Around........ 83

Plitvice Lakes National Park............... 83
Sights............................ 83
◐ Donja jezera................... 84
Gornja jezera.................... 84
Accommodations and Food 84
Getting There and Around........ 84

Murter and the Kornati Islands............. 85
Murter 85
◐ **Kornati Islands**................ 85
Food 86
Getting There and Around........... 86

Šibenik 87
Sights............................ 88

Katedrala svetog Jakova 88
Kneževa palača 88
Trg Republike Hrvatske 89
Srdenjovje kovni samostanski
  mediteranski vrt Sv. Lovre 89
Kaštel svetog Mihovila 89
Etnoland 89
Beaches 90
Entertainment and Events 90
Nightlife 90
Festivals and Events 91
Accommodations 91
Food 91
Information and Services 92
Getting There and Around 92
Around Šibenik 92
Krka National Park 92
Krapanj Island .94
Southeast of Šibenik 94
Primošten 94
Sights 94
Wineries 95
Beaches 95
Accommodations and Food 95
Getting There and Around 95
Trogir 96
Sights 96
Kopnena vrata .96
Katedrala svetog Lovrijenca 96
Čipiko Palace 97
Gradska loža 97
Samostan svetog Nikole 98
Riva 98
Beaches 98
Entertainment and Events 99
Accommodations 99
Food 99
Information and Services 100
Getting There and Around 100
Around Trogir 100
Kaštela 100
Drvenik Mali and Drvenik Veli 100

DUBROVNIK &
THE DALMATIAN COAST

EUGEN DOBRIC © DREAMSTIME.COM

DUBROVNIK

Ragusa. Dubrovnik. No matter what the city's been called over the centuries, it has never failed to inspire. Within Dubrovnik's ancient stone walls lies a tangle of creamy stone structures and quiet little alleyways filled with stunning relics of its past. The city's rich history has created a vibrant cultural and musical scene, with concerts and galleries hiding in the most unexpected places. However, at the height of the summer season, Dubrovnik's glorious past draws thousands of visitors, with large cruise ships docking to release their masses—perhaps not a part of the trip you envisioned.

Of course there are plenty of reasons the tourists continue to pile into town. Chief among them is the sheer beauty of the city, which can be both grand and quaint, melancholy and sun-drenched-happy, depending on the view or the fall of the shadows. The city has impressed generations of holidaymakers, though sadly Dubrovnik's self-confidence often turns into an air of coldness and over-importance, a bit like other once-grand seaside provincial towns. Look past the occasional attitude to the magnificent buildings and island-peppered sea beyond.

Of course, some of the attitude is deserved. Dubrovnik is the crown jewel of Croatia and accounts for a huge bulk of the country's tourist trade—it's the city everyone's heard of. The upsides to all this bustle are the many fine hotels and shops and the breadth of tourist amenities you're likely to find. Of course, it's hard to see the upside when you're jam-packed with fellow travelers or left waiting for a table. When the Stradun gets too crowded, escape to less-visited

© DREAMSTIME.COM

HIGHLIGHTS

◖ **Gradske zidine:** There's not a better way to get an eyeful of the white city and start a tour around the old core of Dubrovnik than a walk along the 15th-century walls (page 12).

◖ **Stradun:** Though it's impossible to miss the Stradun, it's easy to miss its beauty when you're moving along in a river of travelers. Stop for a coffee at one of the cafés to soak in the atmosphere on Dubrovnik's main artery (page 12).

◖ **War Photo Limited:** This moving gallery hosts a permanent exhibition of photographs from Croatia's 1990s Homeland War, as well as work from other regions of the world by renowned photojournalists (page 14).

◖ **Pustijerna:** Dubrovnik's oldest quarter, with many medieval buildings that survived the 1667 earthquake, is also home to the stunning Crkva Sv. Ignacija (page 17).

◖ **Lokrum:** One place to get away from the biggest crowds, this forested island is a nice spot for a swim or a hike (page 19).

◖ **Trsteno:** Fans of formal gardens or those in search of an escape should head to these Renaissance gardens, full of herbs, fruit trees, and languid statues that have inspired many a local poet and writer (page 28).

◖ **Pelješac Peninsula:** Wine lovers and foodies shouldn't miss this excursion near Dubrovnik for oysters, seafood, and a wine crawl (page 30).

LOOK FOR ◖ TO FIND RECOMMENDED SIGHTS, ACTIVITIES, DINING, AND LODGING.

sights around Dubrovnik, like Trsteno—former summer home of Dubrovnik's nobility, the sparsely populated Elafiti Islands, or a winery on the Pelješac Peninsula.

HISTORY

Dubrovnik was originally a small island, inhabited by the Illyrians and the Romans. Its name, historically Ragusa, was first mentioned in 667. At that time it was a refuge for people fleeing invaders that came after the demise of the Roman empire. A Slav settlement sprung up across the channel, called Dubrava. The narrow waterway was filled in between the 10th and 11th centuries, the two cities merged, and the city spread all the way to the foot of Mount Srd.

During the 9th and 10th centuries Dubrovnik was under the control of the Byzantine Empire, which helped protect the port city from invaders. In the 11th century, however, Dubrovnik flipped from Byzantine to Venetian control (in 1000), back to Byzantine (1018), and to the Normans (1081). By the 12th century, Dubrovnik was becoming a powerful and important city-state, signing trade

10   **MOON** DUBROVNIK & THE DALMATIAN COAST

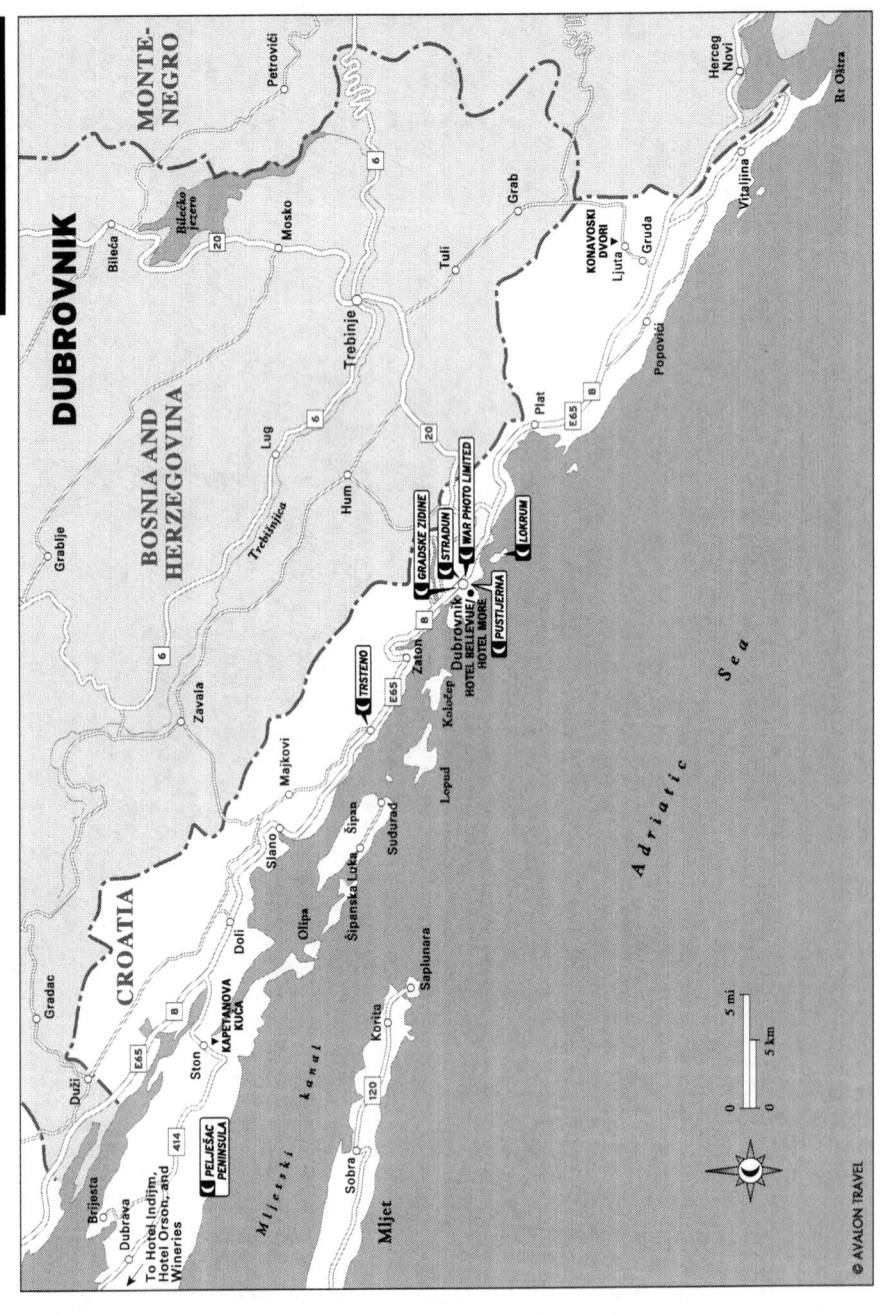

agreements and treaties. In 1189 Dubrovnik, Ragusa's Croatian name, was used for the first time in a trade agreement (though Ragusa was used regularly to refer to the city until the early 20th century).

Dubrovnik's freedom was short-lived, however. Venice once again brought the city under its control in 1232, forcing strict trading restrictions and taxes that severely diminished Dubrovnik's position as an important port. It wasn't until the 13th century, when an armistice from Croatian-Hungarian king Louis I in 1358 made Dubrovnik an independent city-state, the Ragusan Republic. Louis I placed no restrictions on Dubrovnik's trade, even allowing them to do business with Venice and Serbia, often at odds with the Croatian-Hungarian nation.

The prosperity of Dubrovnik changed the city, with the last of its wooden houses being demolished in the early 15th century and the town reconstructed completely out of white stone. Palaces, fountains, towers, a public school, and a shipyard were all built during the town's golden era.

The time of prosperity was brought to an abrupt halt when an earthquake struck in 1667, destroying buildings, killing around 4,000 people (over half the city's population at the time), and pulverizing many pieces of art. The city recovered due to its trade, but its glory days were over. It continued to suffer blows to its position (war with Venice, an unfortunate trade agreement with France, a defeat of the navy by Napoleon's forces) until its status as city-state was taken away by Napoleon's Marshall Marmont in 1808. Six years later Dubrovnik became a part of the Kingdom of Dalmatia, under Austrian rule.

Still, the legend of Dubrovnik continued to permeate among visitors, who raved about the city and began to come in droves by the late 19th and early 20th centuries. It continued to be a frequented destination for visitors throughout its time as a part of Yugoslavia. Though the war left its scars, it was quick to recover tourists based on its legendary reputation and the grand scale of the city that continues to seduce.

PLANNING YOUR TIME

Ideally, you'll have at least three full days in Dubrovnik. Spend the first day with all the other tourists visiting the must-see city sights and the second day relaxing on Lokrum or one of the Elafiti Islands. Spend the third day on a wine crawl on the Pelješac Peninsula, a long but doable day trip from the city. Four full days should be enough to thoroughly see Dubrovnik and its surroundings, leaving you time to scoot to some of the Southern Dalmatian islands like Mljet or Korčula, both with easy connections to the area.

If you don't like waiting for a table in restaurants, try to go outside of the peak lunch and dinner hours (12:30–2 P.M. and 7–9 P.M.). The same goes for tourist sites, as a good portion of the tourists are brought into town from the cruise ships between 9 A.M. and 6 P.M. If some of the places you want to see have wider operating hours, try to slate your visits then, when the bulk of the tourists have gone home.

There's not really any time of year when Dubrovnik is devoid of tourists, though the least will be visiting in the dead of winter (when the vicious *bura* is known to blow) and the most will be in town in July and August. Though the peak season can get a little wild, you do have the advantage of the excellent **Dubrovnik Summer Festival,** packed with classical concerts and theater performances, a must for culture buffs.

ORIENTATION

Dubrovnik stretches its boundaries for over five kilometers along the coast, though the three most important sections for tourists are the Old Town (within the famous city walls) in the center, Lapad to its west, and Ploče to its east. The Old Town is pedestrian-only and likely to occupy the bulk of your visit to Dubrovnik. It's peppered with sightseeing stops, shops, services, restaurants, and even a few places for accommodation. The city is dissected by the all-important Stradun (also referred to as Placa), a wide street running east–west. At the western end of the

Stradun, you'll find the Pile Gate, outside of which buses pick up and drop off and taxis wait for their next fare.

Since many of the city's hotels are located in Lapad and Danče (west of the city but not as far as Lapad), you may find yourself around the Pile Gate often, hopping the #6 bus for the 30-minute ride to Lapad. It's also in this western section where you'll find the majority of the city's better beaches.

The eastern neighborhood of Ploče, once Dubrovnik's cattle market, is a residential suburb with a handful of accommodations and a few more sightseeing stops worth your time.

Sights

Though you can easily get a good overview of Dubrovnik in a day, there's enough here to fill up a few days, lazily wandering through the town's museums and galleries. Make sure to start with the Old Town sights, the best of the bunch.

OLD TOWN
◖ Gradske zidine
City Walls

Taking a walk along Dubrovnik's Gradske zidine (entrance inside the Pile Gate to the left, 9 A.M.–7 P.M. daily in summer, 9 A.M.–3 P.M. daily in winter, backpacks discouraged and prohibited in some sections due to winds, 30Kn) is absolutely the best way to start your tour of the Old Town. Running for about two kilometers, the walk around will take you 1–1.5 hours depending on your speed and the size of the crowds.

Built and tweaked from the mid-15th century until the great earthquake in 1667, the walls feature the rounded **Minčeta fortress** (built in response to the invention of gunpowder) in the northwest, the **Revelin** in the east, **Sveti Ivan** (St. John) by the harbor, and the beautiful **Bokar** (worked on by stone masons Michelozzi and Dalmatinac) in the southwest. The best views are likely from the walls that face the sea, looking towards the red-tiled roofs on one side and the sea on the other. The **Pile Gate,** where most travelers enter into the old core of Dubrovnik, is topped by a somber statue of the town's protector, St. Blasius, welcoming you to town.

◖ Stradun

This is possibly the most important spot in Dubrovnik to explain, given the confusion

---

TWO DAYS IN DUBROVNIK

DAY 1
Head into town early for a coffee on the **Stradun** before it gets too busy and then head out for a tour of Dubrovnik, starting with a walk around the **city walls.** Visit some **galleries** or stop for a quick peek at the **Sponza Palace** and the **Rector's Palace** before breaking for lunch at **Buffet Škola** for one of the city's most famous sandwiches. Continue your tour, saving the **Franciscan monastery** for later in the day when the crowds have tapered off. After refreshing back at your hotel, head to the **Sunset Lounge** for a cocktail and a perfect sunset view over the water. Have dinner at **Proto** and cap off the night with an ice cream along the Stradun.

DAY 2
Today head to the **market** on Gundulićeva poljana for provisions for a beach picnic. From the Old Town's harbor, catch a water taxi to **Lokrum** where you can while away the day lounging on the beach and strolling the shady paths. Splurge on dinner at the phenomenal **Gil's** restaurant under a starlit sky.

SIGHTS 13

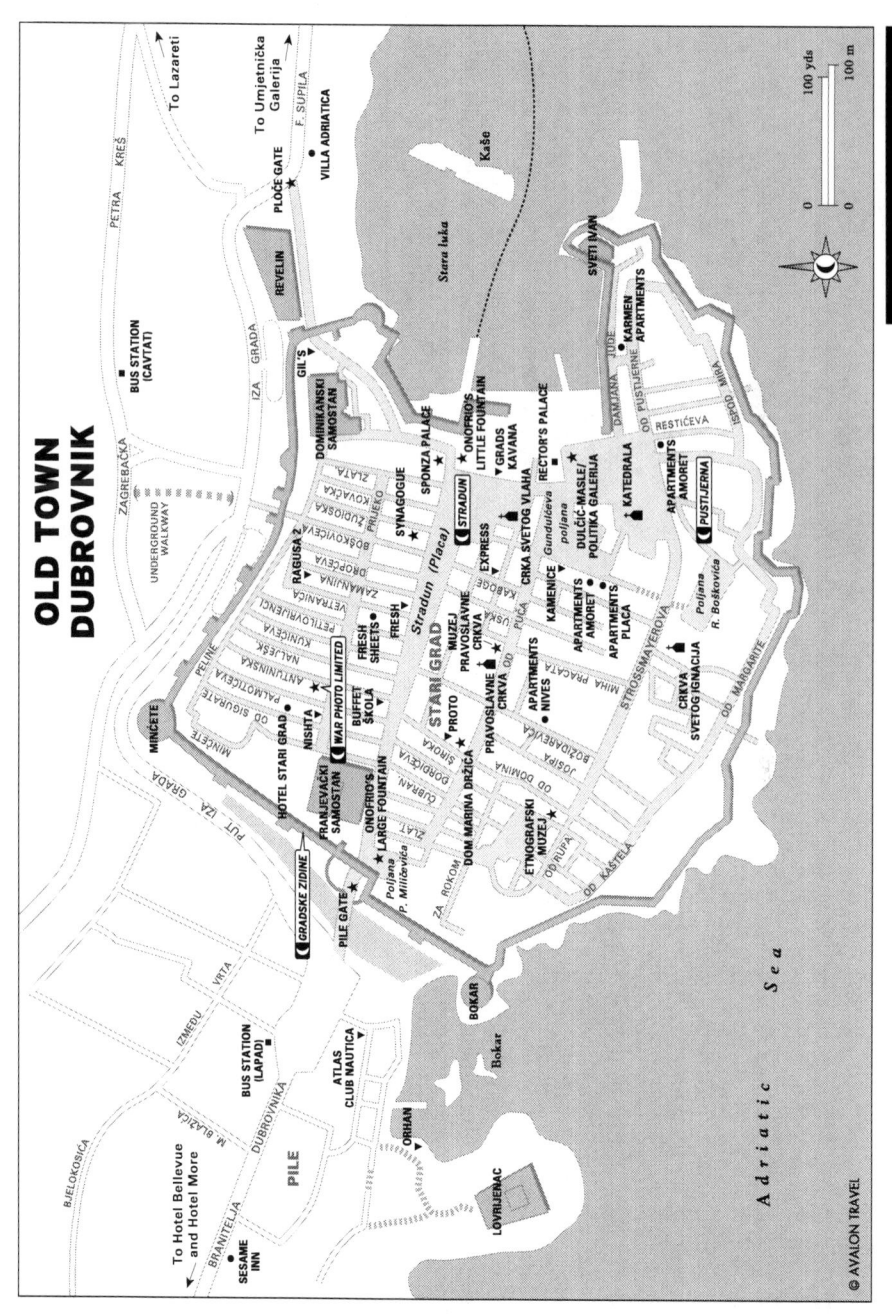

OLD TOWN DUBROVNIK

the Stradun, the Old Town's main street

its name can cause the average tourist—some people call it **Placa** and some use its colloquial name, Stradun. Running from the Pile Gate to the Ploče, the Stradun (or Placa, according to street signs) is the meeting and strutting spot for all of Dubrovnik. It also divides the city into the southern side, Ragusa (derived from the Greek *Laus*, for rock), inhabited by the Illyrians in the 4th century, and Dubrava, on the north, settled several centuries later by the Slavs. The Stradun, which used to be a marshy channel, was filled in the 12th century. In 1438 Onofrio designed a fountain for either end of Dubrovnik's main street. Croatian writer Slobodan Prosperov Novak described the Stradun: "Ragusans see their homes as places where they die of boredom—while Stradun is the place where they live."

Franjevački samostan
Franciscan Monastery
One of highlights of old Dubrovnik, the Franjevački samostan (Placa 2, tel. 020/321-410, www.malabraca.hr, 9 A.M.–6 P.M. daily, 25Kn) is among the city's most popular tourist attractions. The Baroque look of the building was a later addition, making up for severe damage suffered in the earthquake and fire of 1667. One of the only surviving pieces of the original late-15th-century church is the portal, the fire having also destroyed paintings by Caravaggio, Titian, and many others. The cloisters and the monastery's courtyard are perhaps the most beautiful features of the complex, packed with fragrant orange trees. Don't miss the **Old Pharmacy** in the alley between the monastery and the Church of Our Savior. The 700-year-old pharmacy is still frequented by locals today, prescriptions in hand. To battle less of a crowd, try to visit the monastery at the end of the day.

War Photo Limited
A small but moving gallery run by New Zealand war photographer Wade Goddard, War Photo Limited (Antuninska 6, tel. 020/322-166, www.warphotoltd.com, 9 A.M.–9 P.M. daily June–Sept., 10 A.M.–4 P.M. Tues.–Sat. and 10 A.M.–2 P.M. Sun. May and Oct., 30Kn) showcases work by some of the world's

THE SIEGE OF DUBROVNIK

The attack on Dubrovnik by Serb forces came out of nowhere for Dubrovnik's citizens. Not really seen as an important port and with hardly any Serb residents to speak of, Dubrovnik was attacked more to hurt Croatian morale than for any strategic purposes. The people of Dubrovnik were bombed and shot at from November 1991 until May 1992, with the Old Town sustaining plenty of damage. The fortresses of the city walls once again became practical structures as locals hid inside them for shelter and safety. The brave people of Dubrovnik held out and the siege ended in July of 1992, when the Croatian army secured a path to the beautiful city.

top war photojournalists. Permanent displays chronicle the 1990s Homeland War and revolving exhibits bring home to the viewer the grimness of struggles in places such as Africa and Palestine.

Županjska
Jew's Street

The small Županjska is home to a tiny but significant **synagogue** (Županjska 5, tel. 020/321-028, 10 A.M.–8 P.M. daily in summer, 9 A.M.–noon Mon.–Fri. in winter, 10Kn) dating from the 14th century. The Jewish community who founded the synagogue was composed of refugees from the Spanish Inquisition—one of the oldest communities of Sephardic Jews in the Balkans. Inside the synagogue are a Torah, religious texts, and a Moorish carpet all brought by the people fleeing persecution.

Unfortunately, they did not totally escape persecution here either. The people of Dubrovnik regularly ridiculed the Jews, barred them from drinking from all but one fountain, and mocked them in local festivals.

Palača Sponza
Sponza Palace

At the end of the Stradun is the busy Trg Luža (Luža Square). Here you'll find the **gradski zvonik** (town bell tower) built in the 15th century. Most notable among the buildings on the square is the Sponza Palace (Luža, tel. 020/321-032, 9 A.M.–2 P.M. daily, free), a customs house built in 1520. Today the palace is home to the **Državni arhiv u Dubrovniku** (Dubrovnik State Archives, tel. 020/321-032, www.dad.hr, 8 A.M.–3 P.M. Mon.–Fri., 8 A.M.–1 P.M. Sat., 15Kn), containing records back to the first half of the 11th century, with some on revolving display for the public. It also houses a permanent exhibit, the **Spomen soba poginulim dubrovački braniteljima** (Memorial Room of the Defenders of Dubrovnik, 10 A.M.–10 P.M. Mon.–Fri., 8 A.M.–1 P.M. Sat., free) displaying pictures and portraits of those who died during the siege of Dubrovnik.

SVETI VLAHO (ST. BLASIUS)

Sveti Vlaho has been the protector of Dubrovnik since the 11th century. Legend has it that a local religious authority had a vision of the saint that saved them from attack by the Venetians. As you're touring around Dubrovnik keep an eye out for St. Blasius, usually portrayed with a long beard, a tall bishop's hat, and a raised hand with one finger extended as if to make a point. St. Blasius Day is celebrated every February 3 in Dubrovnik, with processions carrying the reliquaries containing his head and a few other body parts.

Crkva svetog Vlaha
St. Blasius's Church

Across from the Sponza Palace, the present Crkva svetog Vlaha (Luža 3, tel. 020/323-462, open to the public morning and evening daily, free) stands on the spot of an earlier Romanesque structure destroyed in the earthquake of 1667. The church you see today, a mass of creamy stone carved with statues, was finished in 1714. Don't miss the sculpture of St. Blasius with a model of Dubrovnik in his hand, a survivor from the previous, and much older, church.

Orlando's Column

In the middle of Luža Square you'll see a relatively unimpressive column carved with a statue of a knight and supporting a flag. Known as Orlando's Column (Orlando was a legendary medieval knight), the monument is much more important to the city than it looks. Considered the most important symbol of freedom for the city, it first had a flag hoisted above it in 1419, celebrating Dubrovnik's position as an independent city-state; it was lowered in 1808 when Napoleon's army marched into town. The statue was blown over by a strong wind in 1825 (even Orlando was no match for the *bura*) and put in storage for some 50 years. When he was returned, he no longer faced east

THE CULT OF ORLANDO

A knight who died in the 8th century, Roland (also known as Orlando) became a superstar of his day when he was immortalized and given legendary qualities in the medieval epic poem *Chanson de Roland* (Song of Roland).

His admirers, mainly northern Europeans, formed a cult, but the fever reached Dubrovnik when Sigismund, the Hungarian and Czech king who would later rule Germany as well, visited the city of Dubrovnik. Orlando was promptly adopted by Dubrovnik as having fought a battle with a Saracen corsair named Spuzente ("bad breath"), even though the battle actually took place long after Roland's death.

---

against the Turks, but north, towards the ruling body that oppressed Dubrovnik's freedom (the Austrians). Today it flies a flag that reads *libertas* (freedom).

Onofrio's Little Fountain

Near Luža Square is Onofrio's Little Fountain, a much smaller work than the giant domed fountain at the other end of the Stradun. The 15th-century fountain is delicate, with decorations of cherubs and frolicking dolphins.

Knežev dvor
Rector's Palace

Though the building is called the Knežev dvor, it was actually more of a government building than a palace for a ruler. The rector wasn't much of a ruler anyway—the title was more honorary than one of real power, as he was given only a one-month term (ineligible for the two years following) and a few apartments in the palace for his living quarters. The palace also held a dungeon that must have made sleeping in the place a bit difficult due to prisoner noise.

The current palace was constructed in the 15th century after a couple of gunpowder explosions (the palace was also used for storing munitions) rendered the old building almost useless. The new palace is a grand affair, with lots of stone carvings and columns along the facade (Dalmatinac, a famous 15th-century stone mason and architect, was among the many craftsmen who worked on the building), the most interesting of which is a relief of Greco-Roman god Asclepius sitting in his pharmacy. The funny part of the story is that locals confused his birthplace Epidaurus (in Greece) with the nearby city of the same name (today Cavtat) and made him its protector.

Inside the palace, the **Gradski muzej** (City Museum, Pred Dvorom 1, tel. 020/321-437, 9 A.M.–6 P.M. daily June–Sept., 9 A.M.–1 P.M. Mon.–Sat. Oct.–May, 35Kn) is largely unimpressive. Sparsely furnished rooms and lots of Baroque (mostly anonymous) paintings decorate the rooms where the rector and other political figures once sat.

courtyard of the Knežev dvor

Galerija Dulčić-Masle-Pulitika
Dulčić-Masle-Pulitika Gallery

Close to the Rector's Palace in a refined Baroque townhouse, the Galerija Dulčić-Masle-Pulitika (Poljana Marina Držića 1, tel. 020/323-172, www.ugdubrovnik.hr, 10 A.M.–8 P.M. Tues.–Sun., 30Kn) is worth visiting for the views over the cathedral as much as it is for the art inside. The 1st floor displays works by the three Dubrovnik artists for whom the gallery is named, while the 2nd floor is home to works by Cavtat artist Vlaho Bukovac and Croatia's famed Ivan Meštrović. By the way, don't throw away your ticket: You'll be able to use it at Umjetnička Galerija in Dubrovnik's Lazareti, saving you about 30Kn.

Katedrala
Cathedral

Although its dome is one of Dubrovnik's postcard views, the Katedrala (Poljana Marina Držića, tel. 020/323-459, 9 A.M.–5:30 P.M. Mon.–Sat., 11 A.M.–5:30 P.M. Sun. as well as mass, 10Kn for treasury) has an interior that is more ho-hum than exciting. The original church, purportedly built by Richard the Lionhearted in the 12th century in return for the kindness he was shown after a shipwreck, was destroyed in the 1667 earthquake. Excavations following a 1979 earthquake uncovered another, possibly Byzantine, church from the 7th or 8th century under the cathedral. The Baroque structure you see today (built between 1672 and 1713) does have a visit-worthy *riznica* (treasury) that houses several oddities, including the arm, head, and lower leg of St. Blaise in a golden Byzantine 11th-century box and a diaper purportedly belonging to baby Jesus.

Tvrđava Sv. Ivan
St. John's Fortress

Near the cathedral, Tvrđava Sv. Ivan is where you'll find a definitely skippable aquarium and the lovely **Pomorski muzej** (Maritime Museum, Tvrđava Sv. Ivan, tel. 020/323-904, 9 A.M.–6 P.M. daily in summer, 9 A.M.–1 P.M. daily in winter, 35Kn), one of Dubrovnik's most important museums. Following the history of the city's seafaring, it has everything from model ships to medicine chests to the blueprints for building the Gruž harbor. Given the importance of the sea to the development of Dubrovnik, it's hard to pass up this stop.

Pustijerna

The Pustijerna is one of Dubrovnik's most ancient quarters, with many buildings dating from before the earthquake of 1667. The neighborhood is quite medieval in feel. Here you'll find the Jesuit **Crkva Sv. Ignacija** (St. Ignatius's Church, Ruđera Boškovića 6, tel. 020/323-500, 7 A.M.–8 P.M. daily, free), a giant Baroque church built in the first half of the 18th century and modeled on the church of Gesù in Rome. The grand staircase leading to it was also inspired by the eternal city, modeled on the Spanish Steps. The steps and the square are often used for performances during the Dubrovnik Summer Festival.

Descending the wide stairway you'll run into **Gundulićeva poljana** (Gundulić Square) where the morning market is held, watched

---

IVAN GUNDULIĆ, POET AND PLAYWRIGHT

Born in 1589 to a wealthy and aristocratic Dubrovnik family, Gundulić began writing plays around 1615; they were performed in front of the Rector's Palace. But Gundulić was not only a playwright and poet. Having studied law, he held numerous political positions in Dubrovnik including judge and senator, though he died too early to be appointed rector, a position given only to men age 50 or older.

The first verse of his most well-known pastoral play, *Dubrava*, serves as an unofficial motto for Dubrovnik: "O lijepa, o draga, o slatka sloboda" ("Oh beautiful, oh beloved, oh sweet freedom").

Ivan Gundulić died in 1638 in Dubrovnik of a high fever.

over by a statue of Croatia's well-loved poet Ivan Gundulić. The reliefs around the statue reflect scenes from one of his most famous works, *Osman,* an epic about the Poles' victory over the Turks.

Od Puča

From Gundulićeva poljana take Od Puča, a street that runs parallel with the Stradun, west to the **Muzej pravoslavne crkve** (Orthodox Church Museum, Od Puča 8, tel. 020/323-283, 9 A.M.–2 P.M. Mon.–Sat., 10Kn). The museum houses a number of delicate icons of Byzantine and Cretan origin. Next door is the Orthodox Church, built in the 19th century.

Close to Od Puča, look for **Iza Roka** (Behind Roc), where you'll come across the Crkva Svetog Roka (Church of St. Roc), not very important but quite interesting for an **inscription** written on the eastern wall of the facade. A grumpy neighbor was obviously tired of some young boys breaking his window during their games and wrote in Latin, "Go in peace, and remember that you will die, you who now are playing ball." Maybe no one had told him about defamation of property?

Nearby is the **Dom Marina Držića** (House of Marin Držić, Široka 7, tel. 020/323-242, 10 A.M.–6 P.M. Tues.–Sun., 35Kn), a Gothic townhome where the slightly eccentric playwright was born in the 16th century. He was constantly at odds with local authorities, as the Dubrovnik of his day didn't think much of his plays and comedies—the only paper regarding Marin Držić in the state archives is a paper regarding a loan. There's not much to see here, but if you happen to catch one of his comedies at the Dubrovnik Summer Festival, where the writer is honored posthumously, and want to know more about him, this is the place to go.

Etnografski muzej Rupe
Rupe Ethnographic Museum

Supposedly the reason to come to the Etnografski muzej Rupe (Od Rupa, tel. 020/412-545, 9 A.M.–6 P.M. daily in summer, 9 A.M.–2 P.M. Mon.–Fri. in winter, 35Kn) is to admire the costumes and relics related to life in the rural areas around Dubrovnik. However, you'll find a stronger reason might be the sweeping views of mountains, sea, and red-tiled roofs from the top-floor display. The building was once the city's granary, a very important location during its heyday when individuals were issued tickets allotting them a certain amount of grain. It's here where they picked up the grain stored in *rupe* (holes), hence the name.

Dominikanski samostan
Dominican Monastery

The somewhat plain exterior of the 14th-century Dominican monastery (Sv. Dominika 4, tel. 020/321-423, 9 A.M.–6 P.M. daily in summer, 9 A.M.–3 P.M. daily in winter, 20Kn) hides an interior decorated with a delicate Gothic and Renaissance cloister and an outstanding collection of paintings by local artists. Included in the exhibit are a painting of Dubrovnik before the great quake and *The Miracle of St. Dominic* by turn-of-the-20th-century Cavtat artist Vlaho Bukovac, as well as works by Titian and Veneziano.

Dubrovnik's Dominican monastery, founded in 1315

CONVENTS IN DUBROVNIK

Dubrovnik's old convents often go unnoticed by the average visitor, though the city was home to eight nunneries before the great earthquake of 1667. Today only two are somewhat preserved – that of St. Catherine (today a music school) and the Clarist convent near Onofrio's large fountain.

Many women were put inside the convents by their elders, aristocrats bent on preserving the purity of their family line. With hardly anyone for them to marry, their parents thought it better to enter a convent than sully the blood with a commoner. The plan backfired – by the late 17th century, the town was already promoting common families to the rank of nobles to make up for the disappearing aristocracy.

Life inside the nunnery was not much better than a prison. A law passed in 1433 required the convents to be surrounded by thick walls without windows and sleeping quarters were locked at night.

One nun, Agnes Beneša, set fire to her convent, possibly to try to escape, in 1620. She was walled up in the Rector's Palace dungeon as a punishment but still managed to wiggle through a hole left for confession and find her way to freedom.

EAST OF THE CITY WALLS
Revelin Fortress

The Revelin Fortress took almost a century to complete, with work ramped up and quickly finished in 1539 due to threats from the Ottoman Empire. Now the Revelin is a concert venue during the Dubrovnik Summer Festival and also houses a café and nightclub. Near the Revelin is the **Ploče Gate,** the eastern entrance to town, which welcomed most of the tradesmen to town in its day. Like the Pile Gate, it's guarded over by a statue of St. Blaise.

Lazareti

Dating from the late 16th century, the buildings of the Lazareti are today part of the modern suburb of Ploče. Most of the neighborhood, which used to be a large market for cattle as well as produce, has been destroyed and paved over. But the Lazareti, built to inspect the health and goods of foreigners before they entered the city, remain untouched. The purpose of the row of gated buildings was not only to protect the health of Dubrovnik's citizens, but also to keep the city from becoming raucous at night and to ferry the tradesmen into town in an orderly fashion.

Today the buildings house the **Art Radionica Lazareti** (Art Workshop Lazareti, 10 A.M.–5 P.M. daily), which displays contemporary art in its Otok gallery, as well as being home to other studios and hosting the occasional concert or party.

Umjetnička Galerija
Dubrovnik Art Gallery

Near the Lazareti you'll find the Umjetnička Galerija (Frana Supila 23, tel. 020/426-590, www.ugdubrovnik.hr, 10 A.M.–6 P.M. Tues.–Sun., 30Kn or show your ticket from the Dulčić-Masle-Pulitika Gallery) in a grand 1930s mansion. There's often an excellent contemporary exhibition on and the gallery brings in a big name from the art world most summers.

OFF THE COAST
Lokrum

Purportedly the island where King Richard the Lionhearted was shipwrecked while returning from a crusade (in 1192 likely due to a late-fall *bura*), the forested island of Lokrum (boats leave the Old Town port, Stara Luka, every 30 minutes in summer, around 50Kn one-way) lies one kilometer off the coast of Dubrovnik. The island was once home to a Benedictine monastery, but it was an Austrian who really shaped the place. In the mid-19th century Archduke Maximilian

> ### ESCAPING THE CROWDS IN DUBROVNIK
>
> In June and July when masses of tourists descend on Dubrovnik from the hotels and from the giant cruise ships that dock in her harbors, the crowds can get to be a little much. There are, of course, out-of-the-way spots around Dubrovnik (head to **Trsteno**) or just off the coast, like the **Elafiti Islands** of **Šipan** (home to over 30 churches, at least six of which date from pre-Roman times), **Koločep** (only 30 minutes by ferry with lots of secluded beaches), and **Lopud** (with plenty of sightseeing and beaches).
>
> On a summer Sunday, head to the village of **Čilipi** (near the airport), where colorful folk performances draw large crowds – but not as large as those strolling the Stradun.
>
> The best tip for escaping the crowds is to visit the Old Town in the **early morning** and the **late evening**, when the critical mass has returned to their cruise ships or their package hotels and you're left to walk around without worrying if you're going to unknowingly whack someone with your backpack.

Ferdinand von Habsburg, brother of Emperor Franz Joseph of Austria, built a summer home on the island as well as a **Botanički vrt** (Botanical Garden), still open to the public free of charge. This is a great place for a swim—there's a nice little lake at the southwest corner of the island—as well as for strolling along the paths that lead to a **napoleonsko utvrđenje** (Napoleonic fort).

BEACHES

The city beach at **Banje**, near the Ploče Gate, is a decent place for a swim, though a much better spot, the beach at **Sveti Jakov**, is a 20-minute walk along the Vlaha Bukovca past Villa Dubrovnik and down a long stairway (remember you'll have to hike back up). It's usually not too crowded and has a superb view of a golden-dipped Dubrovnik at sunset. Remember that hotel beaches are either private or accessed per day for a fee. In return you get to use the beach and the pool, if the hotel has one.

The beach at **Danče,** west of the Old Town, is rocky but quite clean and the **Betina špilja** (accessed via water taxi) is a cave with a nice pebbly beach, though it doesn't have any services or cafés. **Lapad,** west of the Old Town (take bus #6 from the Pile Gate), is also filled with beaches, though it's probably nicer to hop a water taxi to **Lokrum.**

Entertainment, Shopping, and Recreation

ENTERTAINMENT AND EVENTS
Nightlife
If you're capping off a perfect day or beginning a just-as-perfect evening, try the **Sunset Lounge** (Hotel Dubrovnik Palace, Masarykov put 20, tel. 020/430-000, www.dubrovnikpalace.hr, noon–1 A.M. daily) in the Hotel Dubrovnik, a bar that certainly deserves its name. Giant windows allow the sea and surrounding islands to spill into the trendy space serving cocktails, reasonable wines, pricey snacks, and Moet et Chandon for special occasions.

Troubador (Bunićeva poljana 2, tel. 020/323-476, 9 A.M.–3 A.M. daily in summer, 5–11 P.M. daily in winter, no credit cards) is the place to go for summer jazz concerts on the terrace overlooking the cathedral and a too prominently advertised Internet hot spot.

Though there's a slight cheese factor at the hip and trendy **East West beach club** (Banje Beach, Frana Supila, tel. 020/412-220, www.ewdubrovnik.com, 5 P.M.–3 A.M. daily) it's hard to beat the convenience (five minutes' walk from the Old Town), the size, the good drinks menu, and some catchy DJ music.

Lazareti (Lazareti complex, Frana Supila 8, tel. 020/324-633, www.lazareti.du-hr.net, 9 P.M.–4 A.M. when events are scheduled, no credit cards) has more of an edge. Set in the old quarantine barracks of Lazareti, the club hosts live concerts and good DJs throughout the year. Check with the tourist office for a local events guide if the website hasn't been updated recently.

Festivals and Events

The crown jewel of the city's events is the **Dubrovnik Summer Festival** (tel. 020/412-288, info@dubrovnik-festival.hr, www.dubrovnik-festival.hr, 30–200Kn) in July and August, when classical music and plays are performed in eye-catching venues all over town. The festival usually includes a spot of opera and a bit of Shakespeare in addition to the concerts and theater performances of local playwrights like Marin Držić. Dubrovnik usually manages to draw a couple of big international names and these tickets sell out months in advance, some as soon as the schedule comes out in April. If you haven't had that much time to plan, once you get to town you can usually pick up tickets for other performances from festival info booths on the Stradun and at the Pile Gate. During July and August you'll also find a healthy schedule of pop and jazz performances around the Old Town.

The **Libertas Film Festival** (late Aug.–early Sept., www.libertasfilmfestival.com), screening both art films and interesting documentaries, is another Dubrovnik event worth a peek if you're in town at the time.

If you're looking for classical music the rest of the year, try the **Dubrovnik Symphony Orchestra** (tel. 020/417-101, www.dso.hr), which performs in the Revelin Fortress.

SHOPPING

You can shop for books, English magazines and newspapers, and a good selection of books on local topics and history at **Algoritam** (Stradun 8, tel. 020/322-044, www.algoritam.hr, 9 A.M.–8:30 P.M. Mon.–Fri., 9 A.M.–3 P.M. Sat., 10 A.M.–1 P.M. Sun.).

Dubrovnik has more than a few places to buy fun jewelry. The largest is **Đardin** (Miha Pracata 8, entrance on Od Puča, tel. 020/324-744, 9:30 A.M.–6 P.M. Mon.–Fri., 9:30 A.M.–12:30 P.M. Sat.), with masses of necklaces and jewels throughout the many rooms and courtyards of a grand old building. **Ivana Bačura** (Zatarska 3, tel. 091/543-1321, www.ivanabacura.com, 9:30 A.M.–6:30 P.M. Mon.–Fri., 9:30 A.M.–12:30 P.M. Sat.) designs unique silver pieces with contemporary flair. On the high end, **Trinity** (Palmotićeva 2, tel. 020/322-350, www.trinity.hr, 9 A.M.–8 P.M. daily) offers creative designs using precious and semiprecious stones as well as local licensed coral.

If you don't have a lot of time, try **Dubrovačka kuća** (Od sv Dominika, tel. 020/322-092, 9 A.M.–9:30 P.M. Mon.–Sat. and 9 A.M.–7:30 P.M. Sun. in summer, call for winter hours), a one-stop shop selling gourmet souvenirs (liquors, wines, and olive oils), books, posters, and handmade items through its partnership with the Museum of Arts and Crafts in Zagreb.

SPORTS AND RECREATION

To see another side of Dubrovnik it doesn't hurt to unleash your athletic side. Even beginners can take to the seas in a kayak, with a tour to the island of Lokrum through **Adriatic Kayak Tours** (Zrinsko-Frankopanska 6, tel. 020/312-770, www.adriatickayaktours.com). The firm also offers white-water rafting in nearby Montenegro and mountain biking in the Konavle. Scuba divers can check out **Blue Planet Diving** (Masarykov put 20, tel. 091/899-973, www.blueplanet-diving.com) in the Hotel Dubrovnik Palace and **Navis Underwater Explorers** (Copacabana Beach, tel. 020/356-501, www.navisdubrovnik.com) for trips and courses for all levels and interests. For the slightly lower-key adventure-seeker, **Villa Neretva** (Krvavac 2, Metković, tel. 020/672-200. www.restaurant-villa-neretva.hr) offers photo safaris and nature schools in the Neretva River delta, ending with an excellent meal at the family-run restaurant offering equally adventurous dishes of eel and frog.

Accommodations

Dubrovnik is not the cheapest place to find accommodation, especially in the summer months. It also books up early, so it's wise to reserve your room in advance. If you do find yourself in a bind, try one of the agencies that rent private rooms such as **Gulliver** (Obala Stjepana Radića 32, tel. 020/313-313, www.gulliver.hr) across from the ferries or **Atlas** (Svetog Đurđa 1, tel. 020/442-565, www.atlas-croatia.com) near the Pile Gate. Try to avoid people hawking rooms at the ferry terminal and the bus stations, as you'll generally find them way off the beaten track and they often turn out to be giant rip-offs.

INSIDE THE CITY WALLS
Under 700Kn
Fresh Sheets (Vetranićeva 4, tel. 091/896-7509, www.igotfresh.com, 178Kn per person, including breakfast) is clean and friendly, plus it offers free Internet and a convivial travelers' bar. There's also a selection of attractive apartments in the 650Kn to 1,100Kn range if you're traveling as a group. The **Apartments Amoret** (Restićeva 2, tel. 020/324-005, www.dubrovnik-amoret.com, from 640Kn d.) are located in the heart of the Old Town, steps from the Stradun in a 16th-century building. Furnished tastefully with a bit of antique flair, they also have satellite TV, air-conditioning, and wireless Internet. The **Apartments Placa** (Gundulićeva Poljana 5, tel. 091/721-9202, tonci.korculanin@du.htnet.hr, www.dubrovnik-online.com/apartments_placa, from 640Kn d.) front Gundulić Square, the sight of a morning market where you can buy fresh fruits and vegetables for the day. The rooms are bright and sunny with small kitchenettes.

700-1,400Kn
Within the city walls, one street over from the Rector's Palace and next to the hosts' swinging jazz café where Jimi Hendrix once jammed, the **Karmen Apartments** (Bandureva 1, tel. 020/323-433, www.karmendu.tk, 710–1,032Kn) are well decorated and filled with charm. **Apartments Nives** (Nikole Božidarevića 7, tel. 020/323-181, www.dubrovnik-palace.com, 748Kn d.) is another choice, with two small apartments and a tiny room with beamed ceilings, some antiques, and good hospitality.

Over 1,400Kn
The **Hotel Stari Grad** (Od Sigurate 4, tel. 020/322-244, www.hotelstarigrad.com, 1,495Kn d., including breakfast) is in the heart of Old Town. The small rooms and baths are furnished with antiques and the rooftop terrace is a great spot for breakfast or a coffee. However, the number of stairs to get up to bed will not be appreciated by those who've let their fitness slide.

OUTSIDE THE CITY WALLS
Under 700Kn
Slightly west of town in Lapad (hop on bus #6 from the Pile Gate), the **Orka Apartments** (Lapadska obala 11, tel. 020/356-800, www.orkaapartments.com, 425Kn d.) were built in 2007 and offer clean, no-nonsense accommodation a short trip from Dubrovnik. It's only a 10-minute walk to the **Simply Angelic Apartments** (Ploče, tel. 091/911-6901, nena28@vip.hr, www.dubrovnik-online.com/simply_angelic, 496Kn d.), east of the Old Town, which have great views over the sea to the island of Lokrum. The rooms are basic but nice and they are located near a small supermarket, café, and a beach, though those with walking difficulties or knee troubles should beware of the stairs one has to climb to reach the apartments.

700-1,400Kn
Only 150 meters west from the Pile Gate, the three comfy rooms at the **Sesame Inn** (Don Frana Bulica 5, tel. 020/412-910, www.sesame.hr, 1,025Kn d., including breakfast) are also close to a nice beach at Danče and the inn has a

good restaurant as well. Outside the Ploče Gate to the east you'll find the (**Villa Adriatica** (Frana Supila 4, tel. 020/411-962, miroslav.tomsic@du.htnet.hr, www.dubrovnik-online.com/villa_adriatica, 710Kn d.), an early 19th-century family home with one apartment and four rooms. The rooms are sunny and bright, furnished with antiques, and the home has a delightful garden with lemon trees. The **Hotel Zagreb** (Šetalište Kralja Zvonimira 27, tel. 020/438-930, www.hotels-sumratin.com, 995Kn d., including breakfast) in Lapad, west of the Old Town, is located in a sunny refurbished villa with a palm- and cypress-filled garden. The rooms are solidly three-star and the trek to Dubrovnik and the beach is fairly short. Nearby, the small rooms at the **Hotel Lapad** (Lapadska obala 37, tel. 020/432-922, www.hotel-lapad.hr, 1,050Kn d., including breakfast) have been renovated in a minimalist, modern style. The hotel has a small pool area overlooking the sea but no direct access to the beach. Hop on bus #6 at the bus stop across the street for a quick delivery to Dubrovnik's town gates.

The new **Hotel Uvala** (Masarykov put 6, tel. 020/433-580, www.hotelimaestral.com, 1,139Kn d., including breakfast) offers some of the best value for money in Dubrovnik for those who want a hotel with all the trimmings. A few kilometers west of the Old Town in a peaceful location, its features include indoor and outdoor pools, a spa, a macrobiotic restaurant, and wireless Internet access. An equally good use of funds is the **Importanne Resort** (Kardinala Alojzija Stepinca 31, tel. 020/440-100, www.importanneresort.com, 1,139Kn d., including breakfast), an overhaul of four hotels into one property that was reopened in 2007. The hotel has a great beach, two seawater pools, and sports facilities, though it is a 10-minute drive to the city walls.

Over 1,400Kn

The (**Hotel More** (Kardinala Stepinca 33, tel. 020/494-200, www.hotel-more.hr, 1,780Kn d., including breakfast) is close to Lapad, west of the Old Town; the area has lots of restaurants and cafés. The 34-room hotel has a small pool area and a beach at the water's edge. It's about a 20-minute bus ride to the gates of Dubrovnik. Much closer to town is the **Hilton Imperial Dubrovnik** (Marijana Blažića 2, tel. 020/320-320, www.hilton.com, 2,137Kn d., including breakfast), just a quick walk to the Pile Gate. The concierge at the hotel is outstanding and can help you with recommendations, advice, and day trips to the islands. Make sure to ask for a sea-view room, as some actually face a wall. The location of the (**Hotel Bellevue** (Pera Čingrije 7, tel. 020/330-000, www.hotel-bellevue.hr, 2,280Kn d., including breakfast), practically part of a cliff face overlooking the Adriatic, is stunning, as are the well-designed public and private spaces. The hotel has a small beach below and an indoor pool. It's located west of the walls in Danče, so it's a 30-to-40-minute panoramic walk to the Old Town—though with the hotel's chic restaurant and stellar views you may not go out for dinner after all.

Food

Eating in Dubrovnik is rarely cheap and often not as good as what you'll find in other parts of Croatia, particularly in the high season. That said, here are a few best bets that will at least leave you satisfied and possibly even impress you.

CAFÉS AND DESSERTS

The **GradsKavana** (Luža 2, tel. 020/321-414, www.mea-culpa.hr, 8 A.M.–2 A.M. daily in summer, 8 A.M.–11 P.M. daily in winter) offers coffee and cake in a grand Austro-Hungarian space mixed with modern simplicity. Try the café's famous macaroni cake. Another spot for sweets and caffeine is **Dolce Vita** (Nalješkovićeva 1a, tel. 020/321-666, 9 A.M.–midnight daily), located just off the Stradun, with cakes, ice cream, and some decent muffins if you're feeling homesick.

FINE DINING

Ragusa 2 (Zamenjina 12, tel. 020/321-203, www.ragusa2.com, 8 A.M.–midnight daily, 130Kn) has operated in Dubrovnik's city walls for over 35 years. The cozy space has lots of Mediterranean dishes and a selection of 150 wines. Not quite as touristy as some of Dubrovnik's restaurants, Ragusa 2 was honored in a local poll of favorite Croatian restaurants in 2007. Though you'll have to hike up some steps to get there, **Levanat** (Šetalište Niki i Meda Pucića, tel. 020/435-352, 10:30 A.M.–midnight daily, closed Nov.–Feb., 130Kn) near Lapad has nice tables outside or in. Dishes are quite creative, such as the surprisingly good shrimp with honey and sage. Certainly the most fashionable restaurant in town, **Vapor** (Pera Čingrije 7, tel. 020/330-000, noon–3 P.M. and 6–10 P.M. daily, 180Kn) at the Bellevue has a knockout interior by designer Renata Štrok and an amazing view plus sophisticated spins on Mediterranean cuisine. Tops on the list of Dubrovnik's restaurants is **Gil's** (Sv Dominika, tel. 020/322-222, www.gilsdubrovnik.com, noon–midnight daily, 450Kn for three courses), a must-book table. From the

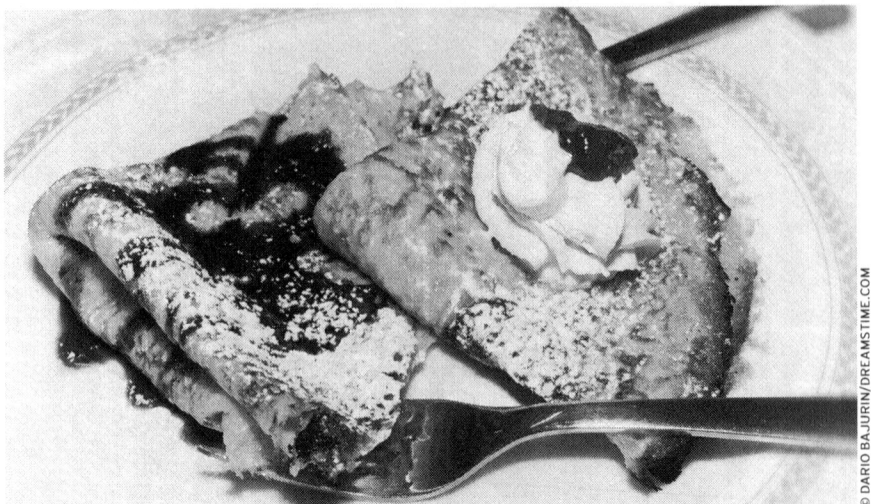

In Dubrovnik, you'll find everything from fine dining to traditional specialties like *palačinke* (crepes).

ROMANTIC DINING OUTSIDE OF DUBROVNIK

For fewer tourists or just for a change of pace, heading out of Dubrovnik for lunch or dinner can be refreshing to both mind and wallet. **Gverović-Orsan** (Stilkovića 43, tel. 020/891-267, www.gverovic-orsan.hr, noon–midnight Mon.-Sat., closed Jan.-Feb., 100Kn), in the fishing village of Zaton Mali, is popular with low-key foodies. Black risotto is the house specialty, while marinated fish carpaccio and the salad of local *motar* (a plant that grows wild near the sea) are not to be missed. You can also take a swim while you're waiting for your meal from the beach in front. Zaton Mali is seven kilometers northwest of Dubrovnik going toward Split on the main coastal road.

In the village of Zaton Veliki, 10 kilometers northwest of Dubrovnik, you'll find the waterfront **Konoba Ankora** (Zaton bb, tel. 020/891-031, 9 A.M.-midnight daily in summer, 95Kn), perfect for a seafood meal at sunset.

Owned by the same group as respected Dubrovnik restaurants Proto and Atlas Club Nautika, **Konavoski Dvori** (Ljuta, Konavle, tel. 020/791-039, www.esculap-teo.hr, noon–midnight daily, 100Kn) is set in a peaceful location next to a rushing brook. Marinated cheese, fresh trout, and meats baked under an iron bell are the specialties of the house. Konavoski Dvori is located in Konavle, 21 kilometers southeast of Dubrovnik going toward Montenegro. If you're driving to Konavle, take the road to Montenegro and when you reach Gruda, take the road for the village of Ljuta, where the restaurant is located.

---

contemporary cuisine (black ravioli with lobster sauce, sushi rolls in foie gras) to the stellar view (overlooking the old harbor) to the wine cellar (with 6,000 bottles), a meal at Gil's is actually worth the money. After dinner head to the terrace lounge bar to kick back with some hip tunes.

QUICK BITES

Quick, filling, and cheap in the center of the Old Town, **Express** (Marojice Kaboge 1, tel. 020/323-994, 10 A.M.–10 P.M. daily, 25Kn) is the place to go for stews and hearty pasta dishes suitable for a backpacking budget. Nestled in a small space off the Stradun, **Buffet Škola** (Antuninska 1, tel. 020/321-096, 8 A.M.–2 A.M. daily in summer, call for winter hours, 40Kn) is famous for its sandwiches on fresh-baked bread and smoked ham and cheese snack plates. **Kamenice** (Gundulićeva poljana 8, tel. 020/323-682, 7 A.M.–midnight daily, 35Kn) is located in one of the most tourist-heavy areas of town beside the market. While it might not get high marks on decor or service, the mussels, oysters, and seafood dishes (all generously sized) are some of the best values in town. Expect to wait 10 to 20 minutes for a table. The **Oliva Pizzeria** (Lučarica 5, tel. 020/324-594, 35Kn) near St. Blaise's serves pasta, salads, and pizza by the slice for only 10Kn. **Fresh** (Vetranićeva 4, tel. 091/896-7509, www.igotfresh.com, 9 A.M.–2 A.M. daily in summer, call for winter hours, 30Kn) offers wrap sandwiches (even a breakfast wrap) and healthy smoothies at tremendously reasonable prices.

SEAFOOD

Proto (Široka 1, tel. 020/323-234, 11 A.M.–11 P.M. daily, 120Kn) has a good Old Town location and a nice terrace, where you should try and reserve a table in summer. The menu is mostly fish with lots of local offerings and even snails. The wine list is solid, too. Proto's big brother, the **Atlas Club Nautika** (Brsalje 3, tel. 020/442-526, noon–midnight daily, closed mid-Dec.–mid-Jan., 600Kn for a five-course meal) holds Dubrovnik's prime position for a restaurant, right next to the Pile Gate with two large terraces overlooking the sea. The best tables are numbers in the thirties on the Penatur terrace or try numbers 56 or 57 on the Lovrijenac terrace. The food here is fancy, like the shrimp soup with black truffles, though it doesn't quite live up to the hype. The view, however, does. Thrifty types might want to opt for a light lunch here instead.

TRADITIONAL

Walk outside the city walls for about 10 minutes, heading west out of the Pile Gate, and you'll find **Tovjerna Sesame** (Dante Alighieria bb, tel. 020/412-910, www.sesame.hr, 8 A.M.–midnight daily, 85Kn). The cozy restaurant serves breakfast as well as reasonable lunches and dinner with dishes like seafood risotto and orange-and-almond crepes for dessert. In the seaside suburb of Lapad, **Blidinje** (Lapadska obala 21, tel. 020/358-794, 9 A.M.–midnight daily, 80Kn) opened in the summer of 2006 with a great location overlooking the Gruž harbor. The meats *ispod peka* are super and should be ordered two to three hours in advance. For walk-ins there are still lots of grilled meats, pastas, and nice pizzas. A short walk from the Pile Gate, the terrace at **Orhan** (Od Tabakarije 1, tel. 020/414-183, www.restaurant-orhan.com, 11 A.M.–midnight daily, 95Kn) is something of an experience itself, nestled between two medieval fortresses overlooking the water. The food is good and reasonable with everything from pasta to seafood to steak on the menu.

VEGETARIAN

Nishta (Prijeko 30, tel. 098/186-7440, www.nishtarestaurant.com, 9 A.M.–midnight Mon.–Sat., 3 P.M.–midnight Sun., 60Kn) offers lots of tasty vegan options right in the Old Town. The vibe is international with a menu offering curries, spring rolls, and wraps. Nishta also doles out non-dairy shakes from its smoothie bar.

Information and Services

TOURS AND TOURIST INFORMATION

Your first stop for information should be the slightly out-of-the-way branch of the Dubrovnik **tourist office** (Ante Starčićeva 7, tel. 020/427-591, www.tzdubrovnik.hr, 8 A.M.–8 P.M. daily in summer, 9 A.M.–4 P.M. Mon.–Fri. and 9 A.M.–1 P.M. Sat. in winter). A short walk from the Pile Gate, the office has much friendlier employees than their colleagues on the Stradun. Stop by to pick up maps, brochures, advice, and free monthly guides to what's on. The tourist office here also has Internet access so you can check your email.

If you'd like a guide to help you navigate the city, **Dubrovnik Walks** (www.dubrovnikwalks.com, May–Oct., 1.5 hours, 90–140Kn) offers two guided walking tours in English (each with two departures daily) between May and the end of October. There's no need to reserve a spot; just show up at the appointed time and place, provided on a convenient map on the website (currently in front of the club Fuego outside the Pile Gate).

COMMUNICATION

Get online at **Net Café** (Prijeko 21, tel. 020/321-025, 9 A.M.–1 A.M. daily in summer, 9 A.M.–11 P.M. daily in winter, 18Kn/1 hour), conveniently located near the Stradun. Snail mail is most easily sent from the main post office (corner of Široka and Od Puča, 9 A.M.–6 P.M. Mon.–Sat.).

OTHER SERVICES

Left luggage can be deposited at the bus station (Put Republike 29, tel. 060/305-070, 5:30 A.M.–9 P.M. daily, 20Kn daily). Two pharmacies, Gruž (Obala Pape Ivana Pavla 9, tel. 020/418-990) and Kod Zvonika (Placa 2, tel. 020/321-133), take turns as the city's designated all-night pharmacy.

Getting There and Around

GETTING THERE
Air
If you're flying into Dubrovnik's airport (tel. 020/773-333, www.airport-dubrovnik.hr), you'll need to find a way to get the 20 or so kilometers from its location southeast in Čilipi to your hotel. Incoming flights operated by Croatia Airlines and British Airways are met by a shuttle bus (30 minutes, 30Kn), which stops near the Pile Gate and at the main bus station near the ferry terminal. On the way back, they leave from the main bus station 1.5 hours before departures. Taxis (dial 970) from the airport will run you in the 300–350Kn range depending on the location of your hotel. You can also arrange for pickup through your accommodation, usually offered for a fare comparable to or slightly less than the taxis.

Bus
By bus (Put Republike 29, tel. 060/305-070, www.libertasdubrovnik.hr, 5:30 A.M.–10:30 P.M. daily) there are almost hourly connections with Split (4.5 hours) and around six connections daily with Zagreb (11 hours); you'll need your passport since a portion of each journey goes through Bosnia. If you're headed to Montenegro, have your passport handy and take a bus that leaves at least once daily. The bay of Kotor, for example, is about a 2.5-hour journey.

From the main bus station, it's about a 30-minute walk to the Old Town, or hop on bus #1A or #3, which will take you to the Pile Gate.

Car
If you're driving to Dubrovnik, keep in mind that you'll have to pass through Bosnia, so keep your passport and papers handy. Dubrovnik is about a 3.5-hour drive (216 km) south of Split and about a seven-hour drive (580 km) south of Zagreb.

Boat
Ferries (harbor tel. 020/418-989) run from the main terminal in Gruž (for Rijeka, Zadar, Split, Montenegro, and the islands) while smaller catamarans and water taxis in the old harbor near the Ploče Gate will take you to Lokrum and Cavtat. In the summers, there are usually two ferries a day to popular destinations like Hvar and Split and multiple connections to Lokrum, Cavtat, and the Elafiti Islands (most islands around 30 minutes, around 25Kn). Winters bring less frequent connections. Check with **Jadroagent** (Obala Stepjana Radića 32, tel. 020/419-000, www.jadrolinija.hr) about tickets, schedules, and prices.

GETTING AROUND
Bus
Around town the city buses (www.libertasdubrovnik.hr) can get you where you need to go. Buy tickets from the newsstands (8Kn) or the driver (10Kn) or pick up a daily pass (25Kn) from the Libertas bus kiosk just outside the Pile Gate. Many of the city's hotels and apartments are located in the western suburb of Lapad. Hop on bus #6 from the Pile Gate to get there.

Taxi
Taxis are usually a slow way of getting around town (the bus is often quicker). Look for one outside the Pile Gate (or call 970); it's 25Kn to start plus 8Kn per kilometer.

Car
You don't really need a car in Dubrovnik—traffic is awful, parking is scarce, and the Old Town, where most of the stuff you'll want to visit is located, is completely pedestrian. That said, Dubrovnik has all the major rent-a-car companies like Budget (Obala Stejana Radića 24, tel. 020/418-998, www.budget.hr) and Hertz (Frana Supila 9, tel. 020/425-000, www.hertz.hr) as well as the fun Rent-A-Smart (Kralja Tomislava 7, tel. 01/487-6172, www.rentasmart.com.hr) located in Lapad.

Boat
Water taxis can be a useful way for getting to some of the area's more hidden beaches and an atmospheric mode of transport as well. Pick them up at the Stara Luka (Old Port).

Around Dubrovnik

◖ TRSTENO

If you're a fan of gardens, you can't miss Trsteno (8 A.M.–8 P.M. daily in summer, 8 A.M.–5 P.M. daily in winter, 15Kn), about 15 kilometers northwest from Dubrovnik. The Gučetić family built the villa and beautiful gardens at Trsteno in the early 16th century. The entrance to the noble landscape is between two ancient plane trees. Filled with Renaissance gardens of lavender and rosemary, fruit trees, and languid statues surrounded by creeping bougainvillea, Trsteno is the ideal place to unwind and enjoy nature. From the end of the garden's palace ruins (which aren't ruins at all, but actually a bit of 19th-century folly architecture) you can grab a nice view of the sea and then go down the stairs to a small stretch of beach for a bit of seaside lounging.

To get there by car, hop on the Magistrala, direction north, and follow the signs. Buses headed to and from Split pick up and drop off here (contact Libertas, www.libertasdubrovnik.com, tel. 0800-1910); the ride is about 40–45 minutes.

CAVTAT

On the Magistrala 20 kilometers to the south of Dubrovnik, Cavtat has a long history intertwined with Dubrovnik. Settled by the Greeks in the 3rd century B.C., the city (then called Epidaurus) was actually a forerunner of Dubrovnik. Attacks by the Slavs in the 7th century forced the people to flee to Dubrovnik (at that time across a channel of water) and abandon the city. Cavtat was later an important fishing village, birthplace of many sea captains and the region's famed painter, Vlaho Bukovac. In the 20th century Cavtat became a tourist destination, with loads of concrete tourist hotels ruining the original beauty of the quiet seaside town. Cavtat is one of the few cities in the Konavle (the area south of Dubrovnik) that was not destroyed in the Homeland War. Its charming old town is worth a visit if you have the time or are looking for somewhere slightly quieter than Dubrovnik.

There are several interesting sightseeing stops in the palm tree–laden old town. A must for book lovers, the **Zbirka Baltazar Bogišić** (Baltazar Bogišić Collection, 9:30 A.M.–1 P.M. Mon.–Sat., 15Kn) displays a collection bequeathed by local scholar Baltazar Bogišić, a great lover of Slavic literature who died in 1908. There are over 20,000 books and manuscripts as well as a wonderful painting by Vlaho Bukovac that depicts the city's carnival—still celebrated in a grand tradition today—with some 80 locals portrayed in their finest costumes around the turn of the 20th century. There's more Vlaho Bukovac at the **Crkva svetog Nikole** (St. Nicholas's Church), with a painting above the main altar, and at the **Vlaho Bukovac Gallery** (Bukovčeva 5, 9 A.M.–1 P.M. and 4–8 P.M. Tues.–Sat., 20Kn), a former residence of the artist that exhibits his portraits (from which he made his living), frescoes he painted on the walls as a teenager, and other paintings, including one with his interpretation of the afterlife. The **Račićev mauzolej** (Račić Mausoleum, 10 A.M.–noon and 5–7 P.M. Mon.–Sat., 5Kn) in the Groblje svetog Roka (St. Roc Cemetery) is another must-see in town. Located at the highest point in the old town behind the **Samostan snježne Gospe** (Monastery of Our Lady of the Snow), the opulent gravesite, built in the 1920s, is one of Ivan Meštrović's finest works. The white stone building guarded by two austere yet tender angels is made even more beautiful by its position among towering cypresses overlooking the sea.

If you find yourself in need of sustenance, try the **Taverna Galija** (Vulićevićeva 1, tel. 020/478-566, www.galija.hr, 110Kn), with a stone terrace and stone-walled interior near the monastery. The menu has something for everyone, from steaming risottos to steak to grilled fish dishes.

Catch one of over a dozen buses that depart Dubrovnik daily for Cavtat (take bus #10), or take a boat from the Stara Luka (Old Port) in Dubrovnik (50Kn). Buses and boats take about 45 minutes.

ELAFITI ISLANDS

The Elafiti (or Elaphite) Islands are a nice escape from the summer hordes of Dubrovnik (though don't expect to find them completely void of tourists, there are just fewer of them). A short ferry ride away from Dubrovnik (from 20 minutes to over an hour depending on which one you choose; check with Jadrolinija, www.jadrolinija.hr, for times and prices), the islands are mostly car-free and full of great beaches for lounging.

Koločep

It takes only 20–30 minutes to reach Koločep, a small green island filled with pines and forests. Historically, the island was known for its coral, though today it's mostly known for being a peaceful spot for a swim. There's a nice sandy beach in **Donje Čelo,** a village at the north end of the island.

Lopud

The boat to Lopud takes a little under an hour and lets off at the island's only village, also named Lopud. Despite the lack of villages, the island is (and always was) the most developed of the Elafiti. Today you'll still see some of the **former sea captains' Gothic homes** around town. West of the harbor and up a set of steps you'll find the remains of the villa belonging to Miho Pracat, a 16th-century sea merchant, who was supposedly the richest man in Dubrovnik at the time. He was also one of the kindest, leaving a giant amount of money to the poor of Dubrovnik. The city thanked him by placing his likeness in a prominent location in the Rector's Palace.

Near the ruins of Pracat's villa you'll find the **Perivoj Đorđić-Mayner** (Đorđić-Mayner Park), a peaceful park, and finally the ruins of a **Tvrđava** (fortress, follow the signs), from whose superb viewpoint you can admire the surroundings.

Locals and tourists alike will agree that **Uvala Šunj,** a sandy beach 20 minutes' walk south of the village, is Lopud's best beach. Near the beach is the **Gospa od Šunja** (Our Lady of Šunj, tel. 020/759-038, open sporadically, free). If the 12th-century church is open, make sure to take a peek at the rather

Lopud, the most developed of the Elafiti Islands

disturbing painting of a large snake swallowing a young child.

Lopud has a good selection of seafood restaurants along the Obala Iva Kuljevana, the town's main street, as well as snack bars on the Šunj beach.

Šipan

While Lopud is the most developed, Šipan is the largest; it's a little over an hour away from Dubrovnik. The island is home to dozens of churches, including several that date from before the 9th century. The first ferry stop is Suđurađ (or Sudjuradj), a village predominated by the giant walled villa of the 16th-century seafaring family Stjepović. Parts of the villa have been restored but are currently only open to tour groups.

If you want to see something the groups likely won't, hike up toward the **Crkva velike Gospe** (Church of Our Lady, two kilometers up), which looks like a fortress, on the hill above town. On the way you'll come across some ruins, once the **Biskupovo** (Bishop's House). Inside is a fresco depicting Michelangelo, who was a friend of the bishop of Dubrovnik Lodovico Beccadelli. Old letters prove that Beccadelli begged his friend to visit him on Šipan, but Michelangelo RSVPed no.

From Suđurađ you can either walk to the village of **Šipanska Luka** on a seven-kilometer road (there are few to no cars on the island so it's quite doable) or get off at the second ferry stop, which debarks at Šipanska Luka. There are some more beautiful sea captains' villas from the 15th and 16th centuries, though the real draw here is the beaches, located on both sides of the harbor (the further you walk, the prettier they get).

You can rent bikes in Šipanska Luka from the **Hotel Šipan** (Šipanska Luka 160, tel. 020/758-000, www.hotel-sipan.hr, 900Kn d., including breakfast, closed Oct.–Apr.). The hotel's restaurant, **Pjat** (tel. 020/758-130, 11 A.M.–midnight daily, 95Kn), offers fusion dishes served on the terrace. There are a couple of other good restaurants in town, such as tourist-oriented (read: English menu) **Tauris** (Šipanska Luka, tel. 020/758-088, www.sipan.info, 8 A.M.–midnight daily, closed Nov.–mid-Apr.) that serves decidedly quality local specialties: fresh fish, fish stew, fish pâté, olive oil, and refreshing salads.

◖ PELJEŠAC PENINSULA

Lying just to the north of Dubrovnik, the Pelješac Peninsula stretches its verdant arm into the sea toward the island of Korčula. It's actually quite remote and a nice respite after all the busyness of Dubrovnik. The peninsula is also a great stop for food and wine lovers, with some of Croatia's best wines being produced in its vineyards. Even from Dubrovnik or Korčula it's possible to fit in a day trip of winery-hopping.

Orebić

A small town that relied heavily on its trading alliance with nearby Dubrovnik for several centuries, Orebić is now home to lots of hotels catering to those who come to enjoy the nice shingle beaches on its shores.

But before you put on your bathing suit, take a peek at the **Franjevački samostan** (Franciscan monastery, 9 A.M.–noon and 5–7 P.M. Mon.–Sat., 5–7 P.M. Sun., 10Kn), about a half-hour walk up the hill out of town. Filled with attractive icons and paintings, most given by sailors in gratitude for safe journeys or rescues, the monastery also has a lovely view of the surroundings from its terrace.

If you're looking for a sandy beach, head 20 minutes east from the ferry terminal to **Trstenica**, great for kids and with plenty of cafés and *konobas* for refreshment.

The **Hotel Orsan** (Kralja Petra Krešimira IV 119, tel. 020/797-800, orebic-htp@du.t-com.hr, 263Kn d., including breakfast) is not fancy, the rooms are quite outdated, and the food's not that great. The upsides? You can walk to town via a waterfront promenade, lounge by the pool, sun on the beach right in front of the hotel, and enjoy the pretty sea views for relatively little money.

For something a bit more chic, try the small boutique **Hotel Indijan** (Škvar 2, tel. 020/714-

555, www.hotelindijan.com, 997Kn d., including breakfast). The modern hotel has a beach right outside, an indoor/outdoor pool, and a solid restaurant if you don't feel like eating out.

For meals try the **Pelješki dvori** (Obala Pomorca 36, tel. 020/713-329, 10 A.M.–midnight daily, closed Nov.–Dec., 95Kn) for decent, though slightly touristy, meats and seafood. The quirkier **Taverna Mlinica** (Obala Pomorca, tel. 020/713-886, call for hours, 190Kn) is more of a local place with specialties like baked octopus and lamb, though the character doesn't come cheap.

Orebić is about a two-hour drive northwest of Dubrovnik. There are several daily buses from Dubrovnik to Orebić (1.5–2 hours), usually continuing on to Korčula. Orebić is also connected by several daily (in summer, less in winter) ferries to the island of Korčula, which take only about 15 minutes.

Ston and Mali Ston

The walled city of Ston, important to the protection of Dubrovnik for centuries, has a pre-Romanesque church just west of town, the **Crkva svetog Mihovila** (St. Michael's Church), that's nice to see. However, the real draw of the area is enjoying a meal of the oysters that come from the beds in nearby Mali Ston (the towns are less than a kilometer apart).

The small family-run hotel **Ostrea** (Mali Ston, tel. 020/754-555, www.ostrea.hr, 710Kn d., including breakfast) is right on the water, with attractively furnished rooms; it's conveniently located right next to the best restaurant in town, Kapetanova kuća, owned by the same family.

Don't leave without trying **Kapetanova kuća** (Mali Ston, tel. 020/754-555, www.ostrea.hr, 9 A.M.–midnight daily, 170Kn) for excellent food including Ston oysters and even octopus burgers. The interior is nice (with the prerequisite stone walls, convivial atmosphere, and neat table settings), but it's the harborside terrace, with a lulling view of the bobbing boats, that might make you drag out your meal as long as possible.

With restaurants in both Split and Zagreb,

the town of Ston, on the Pelješac Peninsula

Bota Šare (Kroz polje 5, tel. 020/754-482, www.bota-sare.hr, 9 A.M.–11 P.M. daily, 100Kn) is known as a reliable source of good seafood. The cozy stone interior in Mali Ston is a plus as well.

Ston and Mali Ston are 60 kilometers northwest of Dubrovnik. Buses traveling from Dubrovnik to Orebić pass through Ston and Mali Ston. They take about 1.5 hours. If you're driving from Dubrovnik, take highway 8 toward Split and take road 414 toward Ston and Mali Ston (it's unlikely you'll notice 414 so it's better to look out for signs for Ston or Orebić). The drive should take about 1.5 hours.

Wineries

Home to some of Croatia's best wineries, the Pelješac Peninsula is the perfect place for a wine crawl through the steep grape-laden vineyards. The peninsula is home to a variety of whites and reds but it's best known for its rich Dingač, a reliable wine that can veer into world-class territory depending on the maker and the year. There are dozens of wineries in the area but it's worthwhile to call out a few of the best. First up is the **Grgić winery** (Trstenik 78, tel. 020/748-090, grgic-vina@du.htnet.hr, 10 A.M.–5 P.M. Mon.–Sat.) in Trstenik, about 15 kilometers east of Orebić, actually the Croatian branch of American Grgich Hills Winery in Napa Valley, California. Mr. Grgić returned to his homeland in the 1990s to start a vineyard that has quickly gained a serious reputation, particularly for its Plavac Mali.

In the village of Potomje, about 10 kilometers east of Orebić, visit **Niko Bura** (tel. 020/742-204, call for hours) for his Dingač Bura and Postup wines as well as **Vedran Kiridzija** (Potemje 40, tel. 020/742-312, call for hours) and **Goran Miličić** (tel. 020/742-031, call for hours) to sample their Dingač varieties.

The area has a marked **wine road** (Pelješki vinski put, Kuna 8, tel. 020/742-139, vinskiput@net.hr), calling out wineries and gastro stops in a neat little package. If you want to go it on your own, try **Dalmatinska kuća** (Borak, tel. 020/748-017, noon–midnight daily, closed Nov.–Mar., 90Kn) for local specialties and a glass of the owner's wine while dining on the restaurant's terrace.

SOUTHERN DALMATIA

As you get deeper into Croatia's Dalmatian coast you realize you're going somewhere quite singular—it's here that you'll find some of the most stunning coastline and picturesque islands of the Adriatic. Cities like Hvar have graced the pages of dozens of magazines and newspaper articles while islands like the beautiful Mljet are significantly less hyped. Split has plenty of historic interest and also serves as a port gateway to most of Croatia's islands. The Makarska Riviera is usually packed with European tourists at its large package hotels, Korčula is a must-see for fans of Dubrovnik, and islands like Vis are perfect for getting away from it all.

The Adriatic's clear blue waters are the main draw here, whether your preferences tend toward island hopping, sunbathing, diving, or dining in restaurants with views worth traveling halfway around the world for. However, all the region's advantages have translated into loads of travelers. There are still out-of-the-way spots to get away from all the tourists, particularly the islands of Mljet, Lastovo, and Vis—but it's worth braving the crowds to get a look at the birthplace of Marco Polo, the pirate stronghold of Omiš, or a riverside meal on the Cetina Gorge, or making a compromise, like the hidden-away-but-popular Senko's, a restaurant located in a tiny hamlet on the shore of the island of Vis.

PLANNING YOUR TIME

To get a really thorough overview of Southern Dalmatia, with time to do some prerequisite lounging on the beach and lingering over a

© SHANN FOUNTAIN ČULO

HIGHLIGHTS

◖ Diocletian's Palace: The palace is impressive not only for its Roman relics, immense size, and art treasures, but also for the fact that it isn't some relic with a rope around it, but a vital part of Split's center. Small apartments, restaurants, bars, shops, and even a couple of hotels occupy the space once held by the despot ruler (page 38).

◖ Galerija Ivana Meštrovića: The family home of Croatia's most famous artist not only houses hundreds of his impressive sculptures and drawings, but the jaunt out to its location on the pine-covered Marjan Peninsula is a great way to spend a couple of hours during a visit to Split (page 40).

◖ Hvar: Hvar's been rated, overrated, and underrated, but what remains is an island with a celebrity-packed nightlife, top-end hotels and restaurants, and a few things you might not have expected. From wineries to small villages and a restaurant without electricity, there's plenty besides the sleek yachting life (page 52).

◖ Vis: A former military base opened to the public in 1989, the tourism trade didn't really even start on Vis until after 2000. It's still the destination for those that want to break from the crowds and step back in time (page 58).

◖ Korčula: Brimming with culture within the walls of Korčula Town (often called a mini-Dubrovnik), the island is also known for its sandy beaches near the village of Lumbarda (page 62).

◖ Mljet: Mljet is a small paradise with two saltwater lakes at its center, one topped with a 12th-century monastery. The island's relative lack of development makes it a great spot for biking (page 66).

LOOK FOR ◖ TO FIND RECOMMENDED SIGHTS, ACTIVITIES, DINING, AND LODGING.

SOUTHERN DALMATIA   35

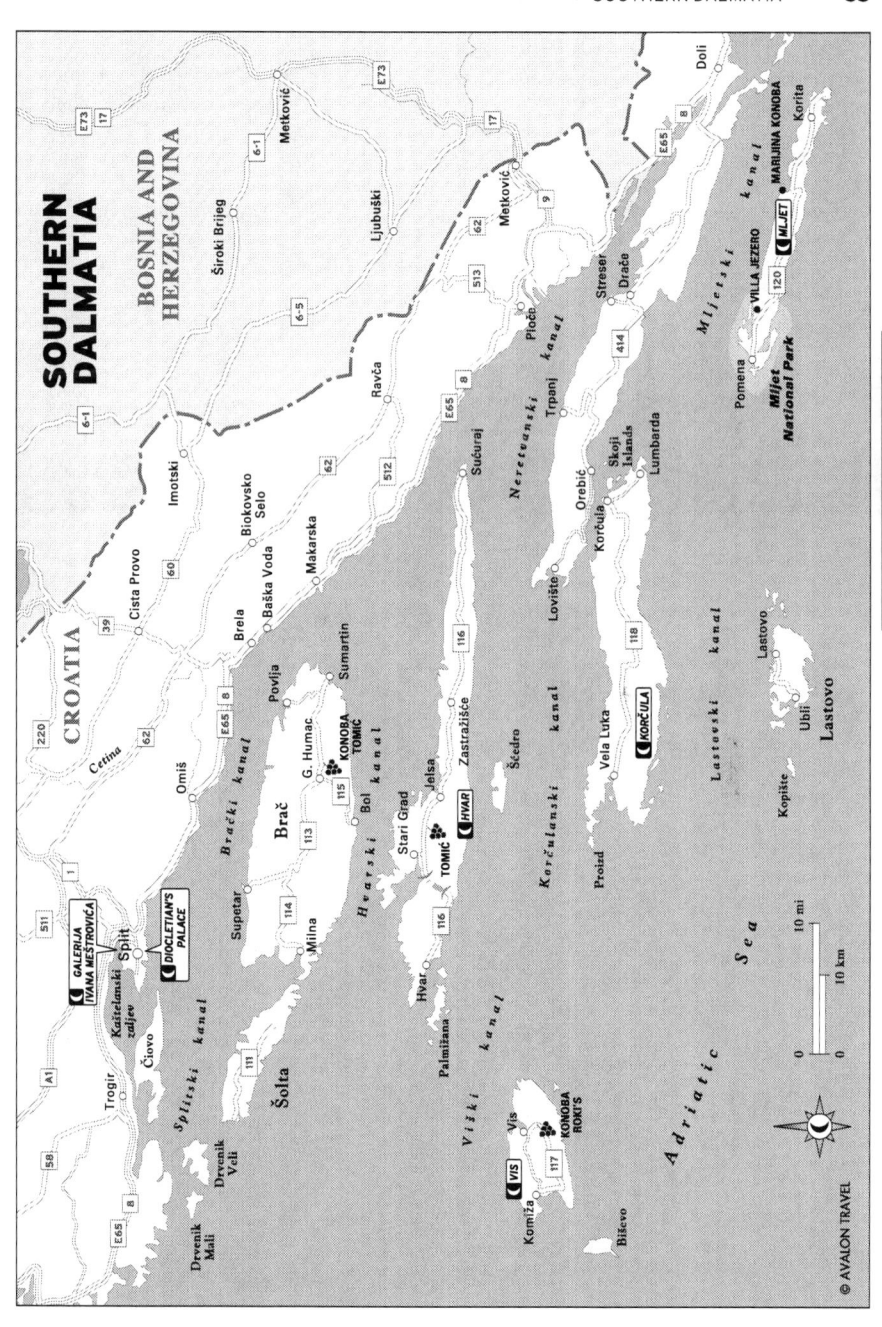

long lunch, you'll need about two weeks. Start your tour in Split, convenient because it's pretty much the departure point for all the islands. Then start an island-hopping tour that fits in as much as you feel comfortable with—doing an island every 48 hours should allow you to visit several while still having time for lounging by the sea. That said, you can take more time in any one place, discovering its nooks and crannies even further until you know exactly which cove is your favorite.

Whatever you choose keep in mind that Split is a must-see (particularly given its convenience) and the other islands should be chosen based on your interests and tastes and not how many times you've read about it in a magazine. All of the islands are stunning and each has its own personality. While it is true you won't find a manicure and a massage or high-thread-count sheets on all of them (if that's your style head straight to Hvar), you will find excellent restaurants, friendly people, and film-worthy sunset views in each and every port.

And don't forget how close you are to Bosnia-Herzegovina when in Southern Dalmatia—it's a great chance to take a day (or even longer) to see another country.

Split

Croatia's second-largest city, home to close to 250,000 people, Split is big and busy, traffic-clogged and even a bit seedy in certain sections. But it's also full of loud and fun people, tons of historic monuments and buildings—a once grand palace at times refined, at times decrepit, surrounded by a network of concrete multistory apartment buildings; half-completed buildings beside garish villas; and a large port ferrying travelers out to the islands.

Whatever your impressions, Split is a don't-miss on your itinerary and one of the most authentic cities on the Dalmatian coast, even in the height of summer. It's a city where the locals still outweigh the tourists and you'll never feel catered to. If you're in town in winter, Split's carnival is a really good one, though not the largest in Croatia. And on May 7 the city celebrates Sveti Duje, the town's patron saint; the whole town takes to the streets to preen and parade. Catch this organic Split while you still can. The city is making big steps to clean up its bustling side—with plans for moving the bus and train stations and replacing worn benches and paving—though it's hard to believe a lot of the city's character won't be lost in the process.

HISTORY

The general consensus has been that Split sprang up around Diocletian's Palace (neighboring Salona was a giant city for its day), built between 295 and 305. But archaeological finds are telling a different story—it seems Romans had settled the area at least as far back as the 2nd century.

After Diocletian died, the palace had various owners, until it became a refuge for citizens of Salona fleeing the Slavs in the 7th century. They moved in and over a thousand years later, people are still living among the palace walls, hanging their laundry out of the windows.

Like most of Dalmatia, Split was ruled by the Venetians from the 15th century, suffered repeated attacks from the Ottoman Empire, and then moved under Austrian rule, when the city became a more important port and factory (mainly shipbuilding) base. The city has really grown due to an influx of immigrants (first from the hills in the hinterland who came to escape extreme poverty after World War II) and then from refugees fleeing neighboring Bosnia-Herzegovina, which received much of the brunt of the Homeland War.

Split is also the home of many of Croatia's biggest stars and athletes—from Wimbledon

SPLIT 37

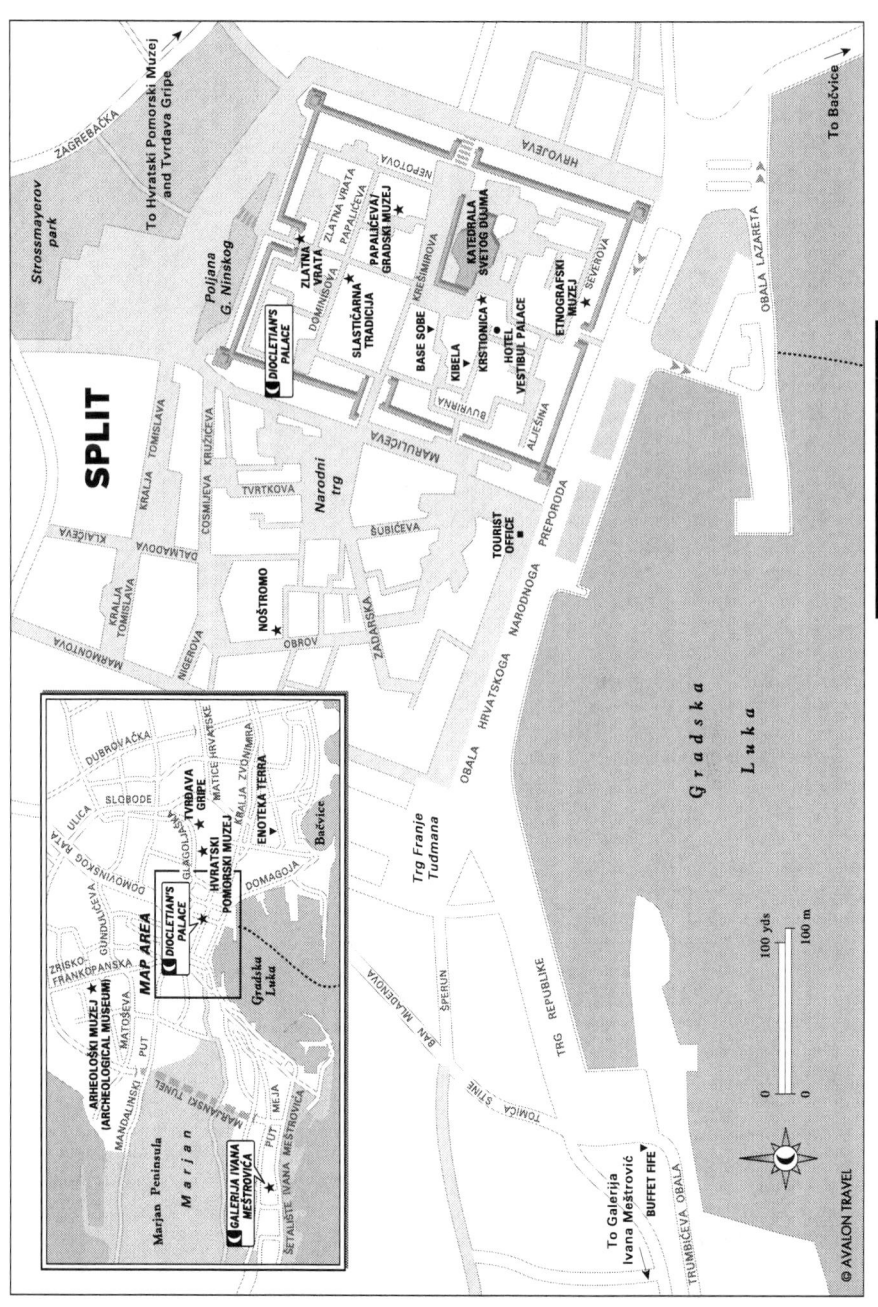

SOUTHERN DALMATIA

winner Ivanisević to soccer players to many of Croatia's biggest singers and musicians.

SIGHTS
Diocletian's Palace
By far the most important of Split's buildings and relics, Diocletian's Palace is almost more of a quarter or a walled city within a city than an actual structure. Declared a UNESCO World Heritage site back in 1979, the late Roman palace itself was reconstructed and built upon many times, so much so that much of the original building remains. The palace is very much in daily use—at least two hotels and dozens of apartments are located within its walls. It was once considered one of the city's worst places to live, but some of the apartments are finding new life with foreigners who pay thousands per square meter to live in a piece of history or as shopfronts catering to the ever-increasing tourist trade. Start your tour at the **Riva** (its lesser-known official name is the Obala hrvatskog naradnog preporoda), Split's center of social activity. From here, you'll pass through the **Porta Aenea** (Brass Gate), which once served as the emperor's access to the sea. To the left of the gate are the *podrumi* (cellars, 8 A.M.–8 P.M. daily in summer, 8 A.M.–noon and 4–7 P.M. in winter, 10Kn) of the palace. These underground chambers serve as a map for reconstructing what the palace was once like above (as the basement exactly mirrored the ground floor), prior to all the renovations. These substructures served for housing people during the Middle Ages, but much older relics have been found, such as a frieze from a 2nd-century temple (likely here before the palace).

On the basement's northern end, you'll find steps leading up to the **Peristil** (Peristyle), today a large square and intersection of the old town's main streets. Surrounded by huge columns and arches, the Peristil was meant for large crowds of Diocletian's adoring subjects to bow before him as he came out through the vestibule from his apartments. In modern times, the square has been a social and sometimes political center in Split. In the late 1960s

Diocletian's Palace

students painted the floor of the Peristil red, a move that angered authorities who labeled it vandalism. In 1998, on the 30th anniversary of the Red Peristil, a black circle was painted on the stones, an artistic statement against the government at the time. Today, the Peristil is often used as a concert venue, for both classical and rock performances.

Katedrala svetog Dujma
Cathedral of St. Domnius
To the east of the Peristil, at the foot of what is today's church belfry, you'll find two lions and a black granite sphinx-like figure to the right. Around 3,500 years old, the sphinx supposedly once had a twin. The building that is today's cathedral was once Diocletian's mausoleum. Octagonal from the outside, the mausoleum is round on the inside, with red granite Corinthian columns. Converted into a Christian church at the beginning of the 5th century, the building became the Katedrala svetog Dujma (7 A.M.–noon and 5–7 P.M. Mon.–Sat., 10Kn) in the 7th century,

> ## EMPEROR DIOCLETIAN
>
> Though he died with the fancy name Gaius Aurelius Valerius Diocletianus, Diocletian was born Diocles, the son of slaves, around A.D. 237. It's possible he was even born in Salona, near Split.
>
> He never did receive much of an education, barely learning to read and write, but his prowess in the Roman military proved to make his fortune. In 284, when the emperor Carus was killed by a bolt of lightning (or by more human means), Diocletian was proclaimed emperor after Numerian, son of Carus, mysteriously died.
>
> Diocletian's first goal was to bring the army under control, which he did, though he became increasingly more like a despot than a Roman emperor. Subjects were required to refer to him as Dominus Noster, or Lord and Master, and he identified himself with Jupiter.
>
> He did, however, split the division of power to some extent by creating a tetrarchy, dividing territories among hand-picked leaders. The tetrarchy worked well at first, until Diocletian retired in 305 – an unheard-of move for an emperor. He had planned for the line of succession to move down the tetrarchy, but the division of power didn't sit so well with the new government. Diocletian died, possibly by his own hand, in Split.

dedicated to one of Diocletian's victims, the bishop of Salona. Huge 13th-century walnut doors depicting the life of Christ serve as the entry to the cathedral. The belfry (same hours as the cathedral, 5Kn), started in the 14th century though it wasn't finished until 1908, is a must-climb if you're willing to trade the effort for some great views of the city. The interior of the cathedral is a heady gilded and marble mix of reliefs, saints, and altars. The most impressive of the altars is the **Altar of St. Anastasius,** where the bones of Domnius are held in a sarcophagus looked over by the stunning and graphic *Flagellation of Christ* by famous stonemason Juraj Dalmatinac. To the right of the delicately wood-carved choir stalls you'll find the treasury, a display of sacral art. Don't leave without looking closely around the dome for the frieze with two medallions thought to be portraits of Diocletian and his wife Prisca. It's believed that Diocletian's body was here for almost two centuries before it disappeared.

Krstionica
Baptistry

Though it's now known as the Krstionica (7 A.M.–noon and 5–7 P.M. Mon.–Sat., 5Kn), this converted building was once the temple of Jupiter in Roman times, likely around the 5th century. Located slightly northwest of the cathedral, it's one of the best-preserved Roman temples in Europe. With an impressive barrel-shaped coffered ceiling covered in reliefs, it's certainly worth a peek. The ceiling, original to the temple, is covered in motifs of flowers and heads that seem to be either laughing or screaming, depending on your interpretation. Turned into a Christian bapistry, the temple also has a simple statue of St. John the Baptist by Meštrović and a cross-shaped baptismal font, decorated with a carving of a Croatian king, probably Krešimir IV or Zvonimir, dating from around the 11th century. The carving was once part of an altar partition in the cathedral and was incorporated into the baptismal font, likely around the 13th century.

Etnografski muzej
Ethnographic Museum

The Etnografski muzej (Severova 1, tel. 021/344-161, www.etnografski-muzej-split .hr, 9 A.M.–9 P.M. Mon.–Fri. and 9 A.M.–1 P.M. Sat. in summer, 9 A.M.–3 P.M. Mon.–Wed. and Fri., 9 A.M.–7 P.M. Thurs., and 9 A.M.–1 P.M. Sat. in winter, 10Kn) was founded in 1910. The stone-enclosed space is filled with various regional costumes and a nice presentation of local trades. The streets past here are best traversed during the day, as it's one of the poorest and shadiest parts of town, long a meeting place for underground transactions.

Papalićeva Palača
Papalić Palace

The 15th-century late-Gothic Papalićeva Palača was built by Juraj Dalmatinac for a local aristocrat. Within the palace is Split's **Gradski muzej** (City Museum, Papalićeva 1, tel. 021/360-171, www.mgst.net, 9 A.M.–9 P.M. Tues.–Fri., 9 A.M.–4 P.M. Sat.–Mon., 10Kn), where Split's history is told in manuscripts, photographs, and artwork. The exhibit also displays fragments of sculptures, old buildings, and a homage to the first Croatian poet, Marko Marulić, who was a friend of the Papalić family and frequent guest at the palace.

Porta Aurea
Golden Gate

On the northern end of the palace complex, you'll reach the Porta Aurea (also called Zlatna vrata), the grandest of the four gates into the palace. The gate is surprisingly intact, save for some missing statues that once filled the empty niches and the columns that surrounded them. It's thought that the pedestals at the top of the wall once held statues of the four tetrarchs (Diocletian, Maximian, Galerius, and Constantius Chlorus). Next to the gate on the outside of the palace you'll find the menacing **statue of Grgur Ninski,** a 10th-century bishop, sculpted by Ivan Meštrović. Unveiled in 1929, the work was meant to commemorate Ninski's fight for the use of Croatian instead of Latin, making it a bit of a national statement. Also next to the Golden Gate, you'll find the miniscule 6th-century **Crkvica Sv. Martina** (Church of St. Martin), once a passage for watchmen guarding the gate and turned into a Christian church in the 9th century. Standing only a little over 1.5 meters wide and 10 meters long, it's likely one of the smallest Catholic churches in the world.

Arheološki muzej
Archaeological Museum

Located just north of the town center, Split's Arheološki muzej (Zrinsko–Frankopanska 25, tel. 021/329-340, www.mdc.hr/split-arheoloski, 9 A.M.–2 P.M. and 4–8 P.M. Mon.–Sat., 20Kn) is the oldest museum in Croatia, founded in 1820. Many artifacts were found in nearby Salona, with thousands of pieces of carved stone, a nice selection of Greek and Roman ceramic and glass, and a courtyard filled with sarcophagi and statues. There are also relics from the Illyrian and medieval periods.

Marjan Peninsula

West of the old town, accessed by walking up Senjska, you'll find the old quarter of **Veli Varoš,** a must-see for those who'd like to get off the beaten path and see a bit of the soul of Split. Here you'll find the **Vidilica** (Nazorov prolaz 1, tel. 021/589-550) café and restaurant, behind which you'll find a small 16th-century Jewish graveyard. From here you're entering the Marjan Peninsula, filled with lush forests and winding paved paths perfect for strolls or bike rides. The green peninsula was actually built in the mid-19th century, when locals started planting pine trees here, and in 1903 even formed an early eco-society called the Marjan Society, which is still responsible for the peninsula's well-being.

The highest point on the peninsula is **Telegrin,** rising some 175 meters above the Adriatic and offering excellent views. Marjan is also home to the 13th-century **Sveti Nikola** (St. Nicholas's Chapel) and the modest **Sveti Jere** (St. Hieronymous's Chapel) backed against a cliff.

It's a 20-minute walk from the center to the **Muzej hrvatskih arheološki spomenika** (Museum of Croatian Archaeological Monuments, Šetalište Ivana Meštrovića 18, tel. 021/323-901, www.mhas-split.hr, 10 A.M.–1 P.M. and 5–8 P.M. Mon.–Fri., 10 A.M.–1 P.M. Sat., 30Kn), founded in 1893, though the current location was opened in 1976. The displays focus on Split's medieval history and the 3,000 pieces on display range from weaponry to jewelry and from tools to sculpture.

Galerija Ivana Meštrovića
Ivan Meštrović Gallery

A short jaunt further down the street will land you at the Galerija Ivana Meštrovića (Šetalište

Ivana Meštrovića 46, tel. 021/340-800, www.mdc.hr/mestrovic, 9 A.M.–7 P.M. Tues.–Sun. in summer, 9 A.M.–4 P.M. Tues.–Sat. and 10 A.M.–3 P.M. Sun. in winter, 30Kn). The huge palace was built by Meštrović, Croatia's most famous sculptor, between 1931 and 1939 as a family home. Though it took him eight years to build, he lived in it less than ten years, from 1932 and 1941, and donated the home to the people in the early 1950s as a gallery of his work. Today the mammoth house displays some 190 sculptures and over 500 drawings from the artist. Near the gallery you'll find the **Kaštelet** (Šetalište Ivana Meštrovića 46, tel. 021/358-185, www.mdc.hr/mestrovic, same hours as gallery, free with gallery admission), originally built as the 16th-century summer home of a local noble family and later used as a quarantine home and a tannery, among other things. Restored by Meštrović in 1939 to be used as a gallery for his 28 wooden reliefs depicting the life of Christ, it serves its intended purpose today resulting in a powerfully moving display no matter what your spiritual inclinations. The museums are definitely worth a visit even if you've never heard of Meštrović.

Bačvice

Officially the city's beach since 1919, Bačvice is not nearly as pretty as some of the island beaches but it will do if you're up for a swim. Given Croatia's Blue Flag Award for cleanliness, the beach is usually crowded with locals, and received a much-needed injection of life in the form of a modern pavilion housing a handful of popular cafés and restaurants. If you notice a bunch of men in Speedos throwing themselves at a small rubber ball, don't be alarmed. It's just *picigin,* a local game with no winners or losers, just a lot of fun.

Tvrđava Gripe
Gripe Fortress

On the northeastern side of town you'll find the Tvrđava Gripe, built in the 17th century to defend the city against the Turks. One of the fortress's former barracks is home to the **Hrvatski pomorski muzej** (Croatian Maritime Museum, Glagoljaška 18, tel. 021/347-788, www.hpms.hr, 9 A.M.–2 P.M. and 5:30–8:30 P.M., 10Kn) with an interesting display of commercial and military seafaring in the area. Costumes, statues, model ships, and old flags are a sample of what you'll find.

ENTERTAINMENT AND EVENTS
Nightlife

Coffee sipping and club hopping are a way of life for Splićani, young and old. Close to the Riva you'll find the eccentric and artsy **Academia Ghetto Club** (Dosud 10, tel. 021/346-879, 10 A.M.–1 A.M. daily) and a more local version, **Po Bota** (Subićeva 2, tel. 098/215-379, 6 P.M.–1 A.M. Mon.–Sat.) close to the Trg braće Radića. It's a smoky, bohemian spot with surprisingly good beer on tap. There are plenty of other bars along the Riva and around, but when they close at one in the morning, head to Bačvice Beach, where **Tropic Club Equador** (no phone, 10 A.M.–2 A.M. daily) packs in bodies on the dance floor, or down the Marjan Peninsula to **Obojena Svetlost** (Šetalište Ivana Meštrovića 35, tel. 021/358-280, noon–3 A.M. daily) with cushy lounging under the palm trees, cuing at the pool table, and dancing in summer to DJ-spun tunes.

Festivals and Events

The best festival in Split is its **Splitsko ljeto** (Split Summer Festival, mid-July–mid-Aug., www.splitsko-ljeto.hr), when theater, classical music, and opera converge on the city; many performances are held in the Peristil.

SHOPPING

There are several spots for wines, oils, and other local gourmet products. Try **Oleoteka Uje** (Marulićeva 1, tel. 021/342-719, www.uje.hr, 10 A.M.–10 P.M. Mon.–Sat., 10 A.M.–5 P.M. Sun.) for a huge selection of olive oils as well as pampering soaps and other Dalmatian goodies. Perhaps one of the best take-homes from Split is a jersey from the local soccer team, Hajduk. The nicest ones can be found at **Cro Fan Shop**

(Trogirska 10, tel. 021/343-096, www.cro-fanshop.com, 10 A.M.–9 P.M. Mon.–Sat.). **Studio Naranča** (Majstora Jurja 5, tel. 021/344-118, 9 A.M.–8 P.M. Mon.–Fri., 9 A.M.–1 P.M. Sat.) is a small gallery showcasing the work of graphic designer Pavo Majić and his wife as well as other Croatian artists and artisans. English books and newspapers can be purchased at **Algoritam** (Bajamontijeva 2, tel. 021/348-030, www.algoritam.hr, 8 A.M.–8:30 P.M. Mon.–Fri., 8 A.M.–1 P.M. Sat.).

SPORTS AND RECREATION
Spectator Sports
There's only one real word you need to know around Split: **Hajduk** (www.hnkhajduk.hr). The local football (soccer) club is more like a religion than a sport. Local fans, who refer to themselves as *torcida,* can be whipped into a frenzy over a victory against their biggest rival, Zagreb's Dinamo. If you'd like to experience the excitement, you can purchase tickets at the office at **Poljud Stadium.**

ACCOMMODATIONS
The **Kamena Lodge** (Don P. Perosa 20, tel. 021/269-910, www.kamenalodge.co.uk, 177Kn d.) is an excellent budget accommodation run by a friendly couple from London. Located in a traditional stone house just outside of Split's center, the hotel has a pool and a minibus service that runs several times daily to the heart of town.

Villa Stina (Na Toc 6, tel. 091/752-5980, www.villa-stina.com, 700Kn d.), a short walk to the beach and the bus and railway stations, has exposed stone walls, comfortably furnished rooms, and plenty of modern creature comforts like satellite television and air-conditioning.

The **Garden Cottages and Apartments Old City** (Solurat 22, tel. 098/171-1730, www.croatiasplitapartments.com, 350Kn d.) are wonderful rooms (with en suite bath) and cottages located a five-minute walk from Diocletian's Palace. The furnishings are rather basic but the surroundings are peaceful and authentic. Make sure to book the apartments and rooms at the Solurat address—the company has a few apartments at a beach location farther away.

Located within the walls of Diocletian's Palace, **C Base Sobe** (Kraj Svetog Ivana 3, tel. 098/234-855, www.base-rooms.com, 496Kn d.) may be the best deal in Split. You can't get more central and the rooms are way better quality than you'd expect for the money.

Five minutes from Diocletian's Palace, **Villa Varoš** (Miljenka Smoje 1, tel. 021/483-469, www.villavaros.hr, 485Kn d.) is a family-owned hotel in a pretty little neighborhood of Split. The simple rooms are extremely clean and tidy and the hotel owns a nearby restaurant where you can grab a reasonable breakfast.

Hotel Slavija (Buvanina 2, tel. 021/323-840, www.hotelslavija.com, 790Kn d., including breakfast) is the oldest hotel in Split, founded at the turn of the 20th century in a 17th-century building in the center of Diocletian's Palace. The history, however, can be traced even further back—there's a preserved Roman spa in the basement of the hotel. The rooms are bland but clean and have air-conditioning and cable TV. Try to avoid the rooms over the narrow alley, where partying-related noise carries on until the wee hours.

The Atrium (Domovinskog rata 49A, tel. 021/200-000, www.hotel-atrium.hr, 1,135Kn d.) is a modern, minimalistic hotel located about a 10-minute walk from the core of ancient Split. If you're tired of old-world charm and exposed stone walls, this might be the place for you. The hotel also has a top-floor spa and pool for a bit of post-sightseeing pampering.

The **Hotel Peristil** (Poljana kraljice Jelene 5, tel. 021/329-070, www.hotelperistil.com, 1,150Kn d.) is a bit on the pricey side for a three-star, relying on its location within Diocletian's Palace to bring in the tourists. The standouts of the hotel are the friendly service and the flat-screen televisions.

The chicest spot in the old town, the **C Hotel Vestibul Palace** (Iza Vestibula 4, tel. 021/329-329, www.vestibulpalace.com, 1,180Kn d.) could have stepped out of an interiors magazine, getting the mix of minimalist modern and ancient architecture just right.

The hotel is small (only seven rooms) and pricey, but then again, how often do you stay in a 1,700-year-old palace?

If you're looking for full service, including restaurant, spa, and a place to moor your yacht, try **Le Meridien Grand Hotel Lav** (Grljevačka 2A, tel. 021/500-500, www.lemeridien.com/split, 1,890Kn d., including breakfast), about six kilometers from Split in the suburb of Podstrana. One of Croatia's few five-star hotels, it pulls out all the stops—an infinity pool, champagne bar, a spa with truffle- and gold-based treatments, foodie-quality restaurants, and of course the marina for dozens of shiny yachts.

FOOD

For a quick snack or dessert, (**Slastičarna Tradicija** (Bosanska 2, tel. 021/361-070, 8 A.M.–11 P.M. Mon.–Sat.) has been doling out cakes and ice creams for over 70 years. Just before Easter, you'll see dozens of locals lining up outside the small bakery, down the alleyway, for *pinca,* a type of bread prerequisite on Easter morning. Best of all, the shop has a special case of "historic" cakes and cookies, like *mandolat* (a cookie made with almonds) and *kotonjada* (quince jelly), once ubiquitous around the area and today rare outside of local homes. Vegans and vegetarians will appreciate **Makrovega** (Leština 2, tel. 021/394-440, www.makrovega.hr, 9 A.M.–7 P.M. Mon.–Fri., 9 A.M.–5 P.M. Sat., no credit cards, 55Kn). The small place has macrobiotic and vegetarian options, with a menu that includes a great selection of soups, salads, mains like burritos and lasagna, and some quite tempting desserts. **Kibela** (Kraj svetog Ivana 3, tel. 021/346-205, 7 A.M.–11 P.M. daily, 80Kn) has been a steady presence on Split's restaurant scene for a quarter of a century, located in an old-quarter alleyway so narrow locals refer to it as "let me pass." Though you won't find it devoid of tourists, the place is a staple for locals as well, particularly for *marenda* and the typical but not stereotypical cuisine the restaurant serves—such as roast spare ribs and hearty bean stew. However, you'll also find a smattering of fish here as well.

If you go to only one *konoba* in Split, though, head to **Buffet Fife** (Trumbićeva obala 11, tel. 021/345-223, 11 A.M.–10 P.M. daily, 60Kn), in the Varoš quarter. It's a simple restaurant that doesn't seem like anything special at first glance, but the food they serve is legendary in Split (just ask a local). It's not fancy by any means—don't look for any truffles here. But if you're looking for daily fisherman's food, a mean *pašticada* on Sundays, and a heavy dose of Split local flavor (particularly in the winter), it doesn't get much better.

Slightly out of the center behind Bačvice Beach, **Enoteka Terra** (Prilaz braće Kaliterna 6, tel. 021/314-800, www.vinoteka.hr, 10 A.M.–midnight Mon.–Sat., 11 A.M.–midnight Sun., 80Kn) has a small but excellent restaurant and a great **wine shop** (8 A.M.–8 P.M. Mon.–Fri., 9 A.M.–1:30 P.M. Sat.) selling a huge selection of Dalmatian and Istrian wines. Terra's *konoba* is a cozy affair—exposed stone walls surround the candlelit tables in the basement of an old building. One of the best restaurants in Split, (**Noštromo** (Kraj Sv Marije 10, tel. 091/405-6666, www.restoran-nostromo.hr, 11 A.M.–11 P.M. daily, no credit cards, 90Kn) and its chef have won multiple national distinctions for their mastery of Dalmatian staples like grilled fish, risottos, and fish soup. The food doesn't come cheap and can't be paid for with a credit card, so hit up the ATM before you come—it's worth the splurge.

INFORMATION AND SERVICES

For information and a few free maps, visit Split's **tourist office** (Peristil bb, tel. 021/345-606, www.visitsplit.com, 9 A.M.–8 P.M. Mon.–Sat. and 9 A.M.–1 P.M. Sun. in summer, 9 A.M.–5 P.M.) on the Peristil.

English books and guides can be purchased at Algoritam (Bajamontijeva 2, tel. 021/348-030, www.algoritam.hr, 8 A.M.–8 P.M. Mon.–Fri., 8 A.M.–1 P.M. Sat.). The main post office (Kralja Tomislava 9, 7 A.M.–8 P.M. Mon.–Sat., 8 A.M.–1 P.M. Sun.) offers mail and telephone services as well as money exchange.

Clean your clothes at a coin-operated

laundry (a rarity in Croatia) (Šperun 1, tel. 021/315-888, 8 A.M.–8 P.M.), only 45Kn for wash and dry, or splurge for their turn-key service (less ironing) for 75Kn per load.

Drop your luggage at Split's bus station (Obala Kneza Domagoja 12, tel. 060/327-327, www.ak-split.hr, 6 A.M.–10 P.M. daily, 3Kn per hour).

GETTING THERE AND AROUND

Split's airport (tel. 021/203-555, www.split-airport.hr) is located 20 kilometers north of town near Trogir. Croatia Airlines runs a reasonable bus (tel. 021/203-119, 30Kn) service to Split. Call the office to check for departure times (they meet all Croatia Airlines flights). You can also take a taxi (try Radio Taxi, 970, or Taxi Riva, tel. 021/347-777). You could hop on a local bus, too, but honestly it's not worth the time or hassle, so we won't explain the hoops you'd need to jump through to get from the airport to Split's center. Wait on the Croatia Airlines bus (only 10Kn more) or splurge on a cab (an alarming 250Kn trip) instead.

Long-distance bus connections are frequent, since Split is one of the main transportation hubs for Dalmatia. The station (Obala Kneza Domagoja 12, tel. 060/327-327, www.ak-split.hr) is located next to the ferry terminal on Split's harbor. There are good connections with Zagreb (over two dozen daily, 8 hours), Dubrovnik (about 12 daily, 5 hours), and Rijeka (about 6 daily, 8 hours). If you're traveling by bus to Dubrovnik, remember you'll need your passport—a portion of the journey goes through Bosnia.

The train (especially fast ones, labeled *brzi*) is a great option for getting to and from Split. Fast trains to Zagreb (about 3 daily, 160Kn) take about six hours, while trains to Šibenik (about 5 connections daily, 2 hours, 45Kn) and Zadar (3–4 connections daily, 4.5 hours, 90Kn) are also convenient. The station (Zlodrina poljana 20, tel. 021/338-525, www.hznet.hr) is a short walk to the harbor or the main bus station.

Split's ferry terminal is a short walk from the Riva and it can take you for day trips to Hvar (1.5 hours) and Brač or a longer trip (around 2 hours) to Vis. Catamarans and hydrofoils, which have the quickest journey times (one hour to Hvar), can be picked up from the Riva. At the marina end of the Riva are kiosks for Jadrolinija (Gat Sveti Duje bb, tel. 021/338-333, www.jadrolinija.hr) and Split Tours (tel. 021/352-533, www.splittours.hr), which also books trips to Ancona in Italy.

Around Split you can rely on walking to get you most anywhere you want to go. Hikes out to the Marjan Peninsula can be circumvented by taking a local bus (#12 from the Trg Republike). A bus ticket will set you back about 10Kn, payable to the driver, or pick one up at newspaper kiosks.

AROUND SPLIT

Largely part of a neighboring suburb of Split, Solin, the ruins of **Salona** (tel. 021/211-538, 9 A.M.–7 P.M. Mon.–Fri., 10 A.M.–7 P.M. Sat., and 4–7 P.M. Sun. June–Sept., 8 A.M.–3 P.M. Mon.–Fri. Oct.–May, 20Kn) are all that's left of a giant city for its time (some 60,000 inhabitants), established around the 2nd century B.C., and an important center of early Christianity. Though many of the prettier statues and pieces were excavated in the 19th century and taken to museums, the remains of the amphitheater, the aqueduct, the bishop's complex, and the Forum are still worth a peek for fans of the Roman period. You can get more information from the **Tourist Board of Solin** (tel. 021/210-048, www.solin-info.com).

You can get to Solin from Split by driving north on the Magistrala toward Trogir or by taking city bus #1. The main information booth and ticket center is just behind the parking lot for Salona.

Omiš

A pretty town at the mouth of the Cetina river gorge, Omiš is most famous for having been a pirate stronghold against mighty Venice in the 13th century. The city is quite stunning: Craggy rocks give way to narrow streets and old stone houses, and finally to the crystal-blue waters of the Adriatic.

SIGHTS

The best sights here are the remains of medieval fortresses built by the nobles of Kačić and Bribir, which harbored the pirates who moored their ships slightly up river. **Mirabela** (8 A.M.–noon and 4:30–8:30 P.M., 10Kn) is the most accessible—just follow the many stairs behind the parish church to climb the tower for a nice view. Further up, the **Fortica** (dawn–dusk, free) is a bit of a hike, about 1.5 hours, for vistas and great photo opportunities.

Omiš has a wonderful **klapa festival** (www.fdk.hr), founded in 1967 and now attracting some 80 groups. The deep a cappella rhythms were once mocked but are now being reclaimed as an integral part of Dalmatian culture. If you'd like to find out more about *klapa* in English, try the website www.klapa-trogir.com.

ACCOMMODATIONS

Private rooms and apartments can be booked through **Active Holidays** (Knezova kačića bb, tel. 021/861-829, www.activeholidays-croatia.com) in Omiš.

There's only one downside to the **Hotel Villa Dvor** (Mosorska 13, tel. 021/863-444, www.hotel-villadvor.hr, 800Kn d., including breakfast): You'll need to climb about 100 stairs to reach the pretty hotel from the parking lot (staff will help you with your bags). If you can get past the climb, the views over stone ruins, the canyon, and the sea are spectacular. The rooms are nicely furnished, though they tend to run on the small side.

the city of Omiš, famed as a medieval pirate stronghold

THE PIRATES OF OMIŠ

The geography of Omiš – large flat rocks that overlook the mouth of the Cetina Gorge on one side and the sea on the other – is to thank or to blame for the pirates that once hung out here. It offered perfect protection for their fleet of light and fast ships that preyed on those who happened to sail by. The Venetians and the Kingdom of Naples, who generally thought they ruled the Adriatic Sea, thought of the city of Omiš as a pirate town. The people of Omiš generally thought they were only extracting tolls from those who were using their part of the sea.

In defense of the Venetians and the Kingdom of Naples, the pirates, ruled by the Kačić Dukes, were quite violent and they weren't altogether fair, even attacking ships heading on crusades, which outraged the Pope and brought Pope Honorius III's fleet into battle with the pirates in 1221. The Kačić won that battle, but a later fight in 1228 pretty much ended their approximately century-long reign of terror.

Hotel Plaža (Trg kralja Tomislava 6, tel. 021/755-260, www.hotelplaza.hr, 936Kn d., including breakfast and dinner) opened in 2007 and has been so popular that during the summer it is difficult to book a room for less than a week. Right on a stretch of sandy beach in town, the hotel is tastefully decorated and has a small spa, and the terrace turns into an ice skating rink in the winter.

FOOD

It's worth the climb to have dinner on the terrace of ⓒ **Villa Dvor's restaurant** (Mosorska 13, tel. 021/863-444, www.hotel-villadvor.hr). Overlooking the Cetina Gorge and the sea, it's particularly beautiful in twilight—you may not even notice the food, good renditions of local Poljica specialties, focusing on meats and vegetables with a few creative takes on traditional fish dishes. One of the best restaurants in the region, the ⓒ **Kaštil Slanica** (tel. 021/862-073, www.radmanove-mlinice.hr) serves excellent local fare (and mouthwatering bread cooked *ispod peka*) with gorgeous river views.

INFORMATION AND SERVICES

The Omiš **tourist office** (Trg kneza Miroslava, tel. 021/861-350, www.tz-omis.hr) can provide you with lots more information, from festival info to rafting excursions.

GETTING THERE AND AROUND

Omiš is about 25 kilometers south of Split. From Split, take bus #60 from the Lazareti bus stop on the Riva or an inter-city bus to Omiš. If you're driving, just follow the Magistrala south from Split.

CETINA GORGE

The Cetina Gorge is full of stunning karst rock formations, dotted with deep-green scraggly forest, and cut through by bright-blue water. You'll find some of the gorge's prettiest scenery just upstream from Omiš. In the summer, boat trips a few kilometers up the gorge are widely advertised at the harbor for very reasonable prices. You can also drive along the gorge, all the way to Zadvarje about a half an hour or so on, where a **vodopad** (waterfall, follow the signs) culminates a nice scenic drive.

Sports and Recreation

One of the best ways to see the gorge is to go on a rafting trip on the Cetina. The trip is pretty mild unless there's been a lot of rain recently. Try **Active Holidays** (Knezova kačića bb, tel. 021/861-829, www.activeholidays-croatia.com) or **Adria Tourist** (Duce, Rogac 1/10, tel. 021/734-016, www.rafting-pinta.com) for booking a trip, which lasts 3–4 hours.

Food

The **Restoran Radmanove Mlinice** (Kanjom cetine, tel. 021/862-073, www.radmanove-mlinice.com, 8 A.M.–midnight daily, closed Nov.–Mar., 85Kn) sits in a peaceful location on the Cetina River about six kilometers from Omiš. Many boat trips end up here anyway, but don't let its tourist popularity throw you off. It's perfect for cooling off on a hot summer's day and for tucking in to fresh trout and frog's legs on the shady terrace.

Makarska Riviera

Packed with tourists in the summer, particularly from neighboring Bosnia, it can be hard to find a spot for your towel on the Makarska Riviera's great pebbly beaches. For the most part, it's a jumble of package hotels, kids looking for a party, and families interested in relaxing by the sea. The area is popular with tourists and day-trippers from neighboring Bosnia as well as Germans and Hungarians spending a couple of weeks in the sun. It is possible to use it as a comfortable overnight stop and offers a handful of hotels and good restaurants. There are also some outstanding beaches, particularly in Brela, though they are best savored outside the busiest months of July and August.

BRELA

South of Split and north of Makarska, Brela is set on a six-kilometer stretch of pebbly beach, rimmed by olive and fig trees. The sea slopes gently here, making it great for young children and hesitant swimmers.

Beaches

Punta Rata is Brela's most popular beach, a long white-pebbled line backed by lots of facilities including restaurants, lifeguards (generally 8 A.M.–8 P.M. in summer), and changing areas. The 400-meter **Berulija** beach has a few more secluded spots, since the coastline dips into three different coves. If you're looking for a romantic beach, **Vrulja** is a hidden cove slightly north of town. The best approach is by boat. You can rent a small one at Brela's marina. Don't be surprised to find a few skinny dippers in the quieter stretches of beach.

Accommodations and Food

The chain of Blue Sun Hotels is the best choice for accommodation in Brela. The **Berulia** (Frankopanska 22, tel. 021/603-190, brela@bluesunhotels.com, www.bluesun hotels.com, 355Kn d., including breakfast) is probably the best value for money. Basic but comfy rooms in the stark modern building overlook a sparkling pool and a gentle slope to the beach. The **Soline** (Trg Gospe od Karmela 1, tel. 021/603-190, brela@ bluesunhotels.com, www.bluesunhotels .com, 640Kn d.), positioned at the upper end of the chain, has swish rooms with wood floors and a giant spa as well as indoor and outdoor pools.

Indoors or out, dining at the **Ivandića Dvori** (Banje 1, tel. 021/618-407, 5 P.M.–1 A.M. daily, 90Kn) is a lovely experience. Sitting on a stone-floored terrace overlooking the water or beside a roaring fire inside in the winter, you can choose from a good variety of grilled fish and meat dishes.

Information and Services

You can pick up information from Brela's **tourist office** (Alojzija Stepinca bb, tel. 021/618-455, www.brela.hr, posted hours are 8 A.M.–9 P.M. daily in summer, 8 A.M.–3 P.M. Mon.–Fri. in winter, but don't stress if you find the door locked).

Getting There and Around

Getting to Brela by car is easy—just follow the Magistrala. By bus it's somewhat more difficult. Buses from Split regularly run to Makarska, though you should alert your driver you want to be dropped off near Brela. If you're trying to catch the bus here, you may need to flag it down to stop, though in the high season you likely won't be the only one waving.

A SIDE TRIP TO BOSNIA-HERZEGOVINA

Just across the border from the Southern Dalmatia coast is Bosnia-Herzegovina (BiH). It would seem wrong to write about Croatia without mentioning **Herzegovina**, where most of the residents are actually Croats. It's right across the border from Dalmatia and you don't even need to bother with changing money, as the locals are happy to accept Croatian kuna. The Catholic pilgrimage site of **Medugorje** is here in the heart of Herzegovina.

Going further into **Bosnia**, you'll find the stunning capital, **Sarajevo**, and **Mostar**, with its dramatic old bridge and lots of Ottoman-influenced touches. If you have time, they're definitely worth the visit, though plan for at least a couple nights. There are still relatively few tourists even during the summer.

If you'd like to visit for a day or longer, you can pass border patrol without a visa if you're a U.S., European Union, Australia, or New Zealand citizen. There are trains from Ploče to Mostar (2 hours) and Sarajevo (4 hours), and buses leave Zagreb, Split, and Dubrovnik daily for Bosnia-Herzegovina's main cities (Dubrovnik to Mostar, 3 hours; Dubrovnik to Sarajevo, 6 hours; Split to Sarajevo, 7 hours; Zagreb to Sarajevo, 9 hours).

Bosnia-Herzegovina is safe except for the large amount of land mines still lying in the fields, so it's best not to go hiking or trekking without a local guide. If you'd like to see the country in more detail or see remote parts of the country without worrying about land mines, contact the excellent ecofriendly tourist agency **GreenVisions** (Radnička bb, Sarajevo, tel. 387-33/717-290, sarajevo@greenvisions.ba, www.greenvisions.ba/gv), a friendly company specializing in guided trips through Bosnia-Herzegovina.

BAŠKA VODA

Low on charm factor but filled with lots of services for tourists (think mid-range hotels, souvenir shops, and loads of postcards), Baška Voda is best as an overnight (or 24 hours) on your way elsewhere.

Accommodations and Food

Rooms at the **Hotel Villa Bacchus** (Obala sv. Nikole 89, tel. 021/695-190, www.hotel-bacchus.hr, 495Kn d.) all have nice mountain or sea views and access to an indoor pool.

Hotel Horizont (Stjepana Radića 2, tel. 021/604-555, www.hoteli-baskavoda.hr, 1,007Kn d., including breakfast) was renovated when the Russian owners took over and now offers fresh but basic rooms, indoor and outdoor pools, and over-the-top spa facilities.

There are plenty of pizza and seafood restaurants along the waterfront, with something for everyone, though without anything likely to impress aspiring gourmets.

Information and Services

The town has a small **tourist office** (Obala svetog Nikole 31, tel. 021/620-713, www.baskavoda.hr, 8 A.M.–9 P.M. daily in summer, call for winter hours) that can help you with advice about the area.

Getting There and Around

There's no proper bus station in town, so some buses traveling from Split to Makarska will drop you conveniently near the water, while others will drop you off on the Magistrala. If it's the latter, you've got about a 15-minute walk into town. Driving, of course, is simple. Just follow the Magistrala south from Split.

MAKARSKA

There's really not anything to see in Makarska besides the beach. It's usually packed in summer, leading the town to have a bustling nightlife.

Makarska's main **beach** is slightly to the west of the center of town, rimmed by loads of package hotels. For fewer crowds rent a boat from the marina or hike from the Riva

Makarska's waterfront

towards the east, where you'll find signed paths leading to **Nugal,** about three kilometers on, where it's much quieter and the scenery is spectacular.

Accommodations and Food

Rooms at the **Dalmacija** (Kralja Petra Krešimira IV bb, tel. 021/615-777, 794Kn d., including breakfast) are extremely simple despite recent renovations, but the hotel is relatively convenient and has swimming pools, a restaurant, and a decent array of facilities.

Though the **Mlinice Boarding House** (Put Mlinica bb, tel. 021/615-889, mlinice@st.htnet.hr, www.makarska-croatia.com/mlinice, 320Kn d., including breakfast) is not on the beach, it's only a two-kilometer (about 30-minute) walk downhill to town. The rooms facing the sea have stunning views and the value for money is quite good for the area. The boarding house also houses a good restaurant if you don't feel like going out again after a long day sunning on the beach.

Restoran Jež (Petra Krešimira IV 90, tel. 021/611-741, 11 A.M.–midnight daily, closed Jan.), literally Hedgehog Restaurant, has long been considered one of Makarska's top spots for fish dishes, seafood appetizers, and a solid wine list.

Information and Services

The town has a helpful **tourist office** (Obala kralja Tomislava bb, tel. 021/612-002, www.makarska.com, 8 A.M.–9 P.M. daily in summer, 9 A.M.–3 P.M. Mon.–Fri. in winter).

Getting There and Around

Makarska's bus station (Ante Starčevića 30, tel. 021/612-333) is only a few minutes' walk to the water. From here you can catch one of several daily buses to Dubrovnik (3 hours) or Split (1.5 hours). Driving to Makarska, just take the Magistrala south from Split.

Southern Dalmatian Islands

BRAČ

Brač is Croatia's third-largest island, and arguably one of its most popular. Stemming from the bustling beach life of towns like Bol and Supetar and fueled by its proximity to the mainland (only one hour), Brač sees thousands of tourists every summer. If you're seeking peace and quiet, though, it's easily found in the semi-abandoned interior. Neglected vineyards are the only remnants of the once large winemaking trade on the island. Many plants succumbed to disease in the early 20th century, forcing winemakers to abandon their fields and their livelihood.

Supetar

Given that Supetar has a fairly small old town, there aren't a lot of visit-worthy sights in town. The best historic sight in Supetar is actually the **town cemetery,** a peaceful cypress-lined park beyond the town's beaches. The impressive sculptures that decorate the graves and mausoleums were carved by two of Croatia's leading 19th- and early 20th-century sculptors, Ivan Rendić and Toma Rosandić.

Supetar is the main tourist center of the island, though, with plenty to keep beachgoers and young families busy. Stretching to the west of Supetar are lots of pebbly beaches with clear water perfect for snorkeling.

The best beach can be found by driving to **Lovrečina Bay,** with a nice beach and the remains of an old basilica.

Campers can check out **Autocamp Supetar** (Ul. Malašnica bb, tel. 021/630-088, 80Kn per person), situated on a beach a couple of kilometers out of town. **Pansion Palute** (Put Pašika 16, tel. 021/631-730, palute@st.htnet.hr, 380Kn d.) is a small family hotel with clean, cozy rooms and air-conditioning.

Aparthotel Bračka Perla (Put Vele Luke, tel. 021/755-530, www.perlacroatia.com, 1,631Kn d.) has eight suites and three rooms, all decorated in bright colors and modern furnishings. At this upmarket stone hotel the pool area is enveloped by comfy wicker loungers. Inside, a fireplace makes for homey dining in cooler weather. The **Villa Adriatica** (Put Vele luke 31, tel. 021/343-806, www.villaadriatica.com, 993Kn d., including breakfast) is a 24-room boutique hotel with plain but fresh rooms and a much more luxe garden and pool area. Nearby the beach, the hotel also has a restaurant and small wellness center.

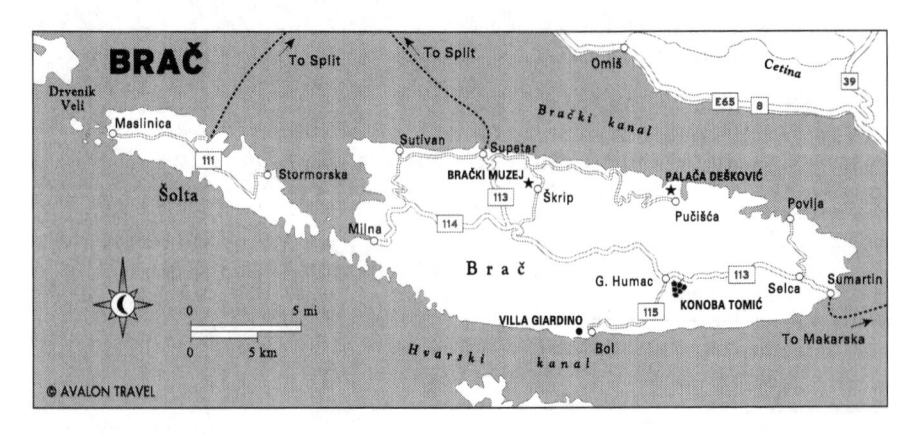

Even if you've come straight off the beach, **Punta** (Punta 1, tel. 021/631-507, www.vilapunta.com, 8:30 A.M.–midnight daily, closed Dec.–Mar., 85Kn) is the sort of place you can plop down for a relaxed lunch. Food is the typical grilled meats and fish, though there are a couple of options for vegetarians as well, and the location is great—a quiet spot a short walk away from the hustle and bustle of busy Supetar. Even quieter is **Restoran Gumonca** (Mirca, tel. 021/630-237, noon–midnight daily, no credit cards, 75Kn), located in the peaceful village of Mirca three kilometers from Supetar.

Vinotoka (Jobova 6, tel. 021/630-969, noon–midnight daily, 90Kn) is a family restaurant in Supetar. In addition to the seafood dishes, be sure to sample some of the owners' homemade olive oil and wines.

Bol

The popular resort town of Bol has two sightworthy stops. The first is the **Branislav Dešković Gallery** (Porat b. pomoraca bb, tel. 021/635-270, call for hours and prices, which vary according to exhibit), a modest museum that manages to include some of the biggest names in 20th-century Croatian art. Bol is also home to a 15th-century **Dominikanski samostan** (Dominican monastery, 10 A.M.–noon and 5–8 P.M. Mon.–Sat. in summer, mass only rest of year, 15Kn) that looks out over the town. Inside you'll find some Greek artifacts and a tender painting by Tintoretto, the *Madonna with Child*. The gardens here are also worth a peek.

But the biggest draws to Bol are the beaches, most notably **Zlatni Rat** (Golden Horn), a long stretch of tiny-pebble beach known for windsurfing and a partying crowd. To get there, just follow the path west of the center. It's about a 20-minute walk; once there you'll find cafés and basic services. If you're interested in a full-body tan visit the more remote **Pakleni naturist beach** (clothing optional) on the western end of Zlatni Rat.

Among package-hotel destinations, the **Hotel Borak** (Zlatni Rat d.d., tel. 021/635-210, www.bluesunhotels.com, 1,060Kn d., including breakfast) is a good choice, located steps from Zlatni Rat with large outdoor pools, tennis courts, and children's activities, though rooms are still stuck in a 1980s hotel time warp.

The **tourist office** (Bol harbor, tel. 021/635-638, www.bol.hr) has free maps as well as a brochure outlining private accommodation around the town, probably the right choice for budget travelers.

Possibly the best value for money in Bol, the **Villa Giardino** (Novi put 2, tel. 021/635-900, www.dalmacija.net/bol/villagiardino, no credit cards, 700Kn d.) truly lives up to its villa status. Tastefully furnished antique-filled rooms, a genteel garden, and ceiling fans (though it has air-conditioning too) deck out the old home where Emperor Franz Joseph once laid his head (in room no. 4).

Overhauled in 2008, the **Hotel Kaštil** (Frane Radića 1, tel. 021/635-995, www.kastil.hr, 740Kn d., including breakfast) has a convenient waterfront location in an old building. Most of the plainly furnished but brand-new rooms have sea views. The building also houses two hotel-owned restaurants and a bustling bar, which make for plenty of late-night noise.

A homey, rustic atmosphere describes **Konoba Gust** (Radićeva 14, tel. 021/635-911, www.konobagust-bol.com, noon–2 A.M. daily, closed Nov.–late Mar., no credit cards, 90Kn), known for its *gregada* (fish stew), *pašticada* (beef stew), and surprisingly upscale offering of regional wines.

Savor fish hot off the grill at **Konoba Mlin** (Ante Starčevića 11, tel. 021/635-376, 5 P.M.–midnight daily, closed Nov.–Apr., 75Kn), a 19th-century mill a short way from the marina. Its cozy terraces are the perfect spot to enjoy a leisurely meal.

Definitely one of Bol's pricier establishments, **Ribarska kućica** (Ante Starčevića, tel. 021/635-033, www.ribarska-kucica.com, 10 A.M.–midnight daily, closed Nov.–May, no credit cards, 135Kn) delivers your money's worth on seaside terraces with amazing views of the blue water and craggy coastline of the island. And the food—fish carpaccio, frogfish with smoked ham, steaks—is sophisticated and well prepared.

Around Brač

A short drive from Supetar (or take one of the three daily buses) you'll find the village of **Škrip,** an ancient village that's home to the **Brački muzej** (Museum of Brač, check with the tourist office in Supetar for hours and prices, tel. 021/630-551, www.supetar.hr). The small museum has an interesting collection of Roman artifacts and a small Roman mausoleum outside, where locals claim one of Diocletian's relatives is buried.

If you're traveling with friends, **Limunovo Drvo** (Bunta, Sutivan, tel. 44-1225/865-591 (UK), www.croatiancottage.co.uk, £800 per week in high season, accommodates up to 11), whose name translates to lemon tree, is a charming rental villa in the village of Sutivan.

The most luxe hotel on Brač, the 15th-century **◖ Palača Dešković** (Pučišća, tel. 021/778-240, www.palaca-deskovic.com, 1,702Kn d., including breakfast) has all the amenities you'd expect from a fine boutique hotel, plus a library and games room, a good restaurant, an art gallery and studio, and parking spaces for cars or yachts.

Wineries

◖ Konoba Tomić (Gornji Humac, tel. 021/647-228, www.konobatomic.com, 5 P.M.–midnight daily, closed Nov.–Apr., no credit cards, 95Kn) is a family-run restaurant and winery, located in their 800-year-old farmhouse in the village of Humac. The family sells their wines all over Croatia as well as in the restaurant, which also offers lots of homegrown, homemade, and fresh-from-the-sea delicacies, like wind-cured *pršut* and octopus cooked *ispod peka*. If you're lucky enough to visit in the autumn, you can see the family making wine.

Getting There and Around

Brač is most often accessed via ferries from the Split mainland (1 hour); they dock at Supetar. Jadrolinija (tel. 021/631-357, www.jadrolinija.hr) and Split Tours (tel. 021/352-481, www.splittours.hr) run close to two dozen ferries a day in the high season. There's also a catamaran (run by Jadrolinija) linking Split with Bol and a small airport (tel. 021/631-370, www.airport-brac.hr) a few miles from Bol that connects to Zagreb.

Around the island, buses (station is east of the harbor, tel. 021/631-122) link Supetar with Bol, Milna, and Sumartin.

◖ HVAR

If you're looking for a quiet Dalmatian experience, Hvar Town is not what you're searching for. But that said, Hvar has advantages that brought the tourists, and the services those tourists have demanded have increased the town's advantages. It's one of the few places in Dalmatia where you'll find multiple chic bars, hotels, and restaurants, loads of yachts, and the occasional celebrity sighting. The island is fairly young, drawing foreigners and locals alike, though more and more Croatians are being priced out of their own playground. Year after year newspaper articles decry the outrageous prices of burgers, beer, and a simple coffee, which in Hvar's summer season can easily run 30Kn.

However, there are a few spots to escape the crazy prices and crowds so that you can have the best of both worlds, choosing where you want to go and when depending on your mood.

Hvar Town

Most of the year, Hvar Town is a quiet fishing village with about 3,000 residents. But by the time July swings around, tourists are descending on the place at a rate of about 30,000 a day. This translates into packed bars and restaurants and lots of jockeying to be noticed by seriously fashion-coordinated young people. But before you worry about the nightlife, there are a few things to see during the daylight hours as well.

Hvar Town was sacked by the Turks in the late 16th century, and the island capital was rebuilt by the Venetians in the early 17th century. Its hub is the the **Trg sv Stjepana,** known as the **Pjaca** (pronounced like piazza). The square's namesake is the church at the eastern end, the **Katedrala sveti Stjepan**

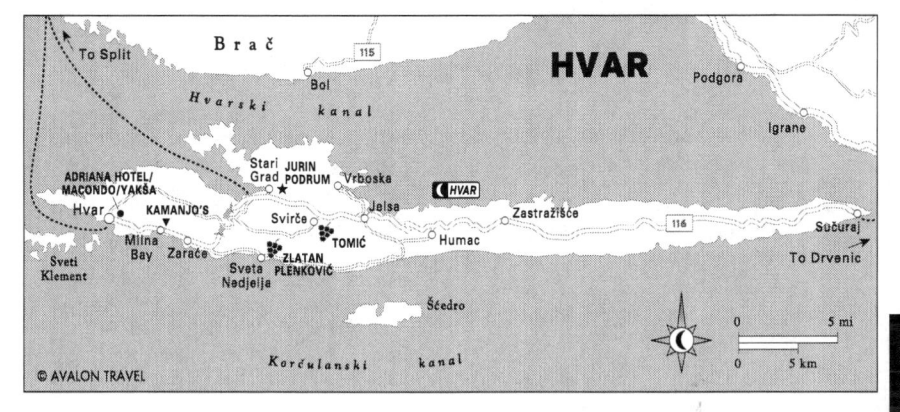

(St. Stephen's Cathedral, open most mornings and for mass), with its very Venetian-style belfry, though its inspiration actually came from Korčula's cathedral. The interior, which has no set opening hours, shelters a pretty Venetian painting of the Madonna and Child from the early 13th century. Next to the church you'll find the *riznica* (Bishop's Treasury, 9 A.M.–noon and 5–7 P.M. in summer, 10 A.M.–noon in winter, 15Kn), displaying a colorful array of liturgical vestments and sacral art.

The square is flanked on its southern side by the Arsenal, built in the early 16th century. A **theater** (10 A.M.–noon and 5–11 P.M. June–Sept., 10 A.M.–noon rest of year, 20Kn including admission to the gallery) was built in the Arsenal in 1612. It was one of the first theaters of its day open to the general public; the present interior dates from the 19th century. Next door is the **Arsenal Gallery of Modern Art** (tel. 021/741-009, 10 A.M.–noon and 7–11 P.M. June–Sept., 10 A.M.–noon rest of year, 20Kn including admission to the theater), which displays works by contemporary local artists.

The northern end of the old town within the city walls is referred to as the **Groda**. Here you'll find the **Crkva svetog Duha** (Church of the Holy Spirit), whose facade was decorated with fragments from other Hvar churches and the **Crkva svetog Kozme i Damjana** (Church of Sts. Cosmos and Damian), the oldest church in town. Its pretty carved Baroque roof is well worth a look. Many of the houses in the Groda were built between the 14th and 17th centuries, though two stand out from the rest: the shell of the never-completed **Užičić Palace** (often mistakenly referred to as the Hektorović Palace) and the **Leporini Palace** (identifiable by the rabbit carving on its facade). Both palaces are located on Matije Ivanića.

From Groda, follow Ivanića until you arrive at a winding path, which leads to the **Fortica** (Fortress, 8 A.M.–midnight June–Sept., 9 A.M.–dusk Oct.–May, 10Kn). The Fortica is often referred to by locals as the Španjola, since the Spanish helped the Venetians construct it in the 16th century. On a clear day there's a great view from here all the way to Vis.

ENTERTAINMENT

Hvar Town's best-known bar is certainly **Carpe Diem** (Riva, tel. 021/742-369, www.carpe-diem-hvar.com, 9 A.M.–3 A.M. daily in summer, 9 A.M.–midnight daily in winter), a frequent haunt of the beautiful, the wealthy, and the famous (at least a few seem to get snapped here every summer). You'll need to reserve a table in the morning if you want to hang here at night. A younger crowd piles into **Veneranda** (east of Hvar's near the Hotel Delfin, no phone, 10 P.M.–5 A.M. daily in summer), a spring-break sort of place with a swimming pool and gyrating house dancers. In the summer there's a steep cover charge (100Kn) due to the place's popularity.

Mellower evenings can be had at the **Pršuta**

HVAR OFF THE BEATEN PATH

Hvar can get quite crowded in the peak season, and if you were looking for sleepy fishing villages and almost-secluded rocky beaches, sometimes the throngs can really to get to you. Try the following spots on Hvar for a taste of peace and quiet away from all the buzz along Hvar Town's streets.

- The island of **Palmižana** just off the coast of Hvar Town is not completely quiet — it's host to fashion shows and art exhibits in season — but it's full of lush forests and gardens, created at the turn of the 20th century by Eugen Meneghello, who also opened up his namesake hotel, today with 14 romantic bungalows and a great restaurant.
- **Jelsa** and **Stari Grad** are both less touristed, yet no less interesting, than Hvar Town. And why not explore the tiny villages, like the remote port of **Sućuraj** or charming **Sveta Nedelja**, if you have a car and really want to get away? Hire a moped or car from **Luka Rent** on Hvar Town's harbor.
- You'll need to walk for close to an hour to get from the center of Hvar Town to **Robinson** on Mekičevića Bay, but it's well worth the trek. The restaurant has no water or electricity but it's a great place to eat (all organic, fresh-catch, and homegrown products) and bathe in the bay out front.
- It's not undiscovered but it's totally unpretentious — **Kamanjo's** restaurant on Milna Bay is a small affair. Make sure to try some of their homemade brandies, signature pastas, and other Italian-influenced dishes, like beef risotto with saffron.

Tri Wine Bar (Petra Hektorovića, Groda, tel. 098/969-6193, 6 P.M.–2:30 A.M. daily in summer, call for winter hours), with over 50 open bottles behind the bar for a wide selection of wines by the glass. It's the perfect place to try local wines.

ACCOMMODATIONS

Only five minutes' walk to the beach or to the center of Hvar Town, **House Gordana** (Glavica bb, tel. 021/742-182, www.house-gordana-hvar.com, 355Kn d.) is a bit like staying at a friendly grandmother's house, and the price is right as well. Also a short walk from town or the shore, **Apartments Ana Dujmovic** (Zastup bb, tel. 021/742-010, www.hvar-croatia.com/dujmovic, 567Kn d.) are bright and sunny, many with balconies. The 14th-century **Villa Nora** (Petra Hektorovića, tel. 021/742-498, www.hvar.netfirms.com, 1,450Kn d., including breakfast) has all the modern conveniences like Internet and air-conditioning in a central location.

Hotel Riva (Riva, tel. 021/750-100, www.suncanihvar.com, 2,482Kn d., including breakfast) is one of Hvar's best (or at least one of the first upscale hotels), set in a century-old stone building right on the busy Riva. Minimalist rooms are accented with bright red and oversized photos of legendary screen stars. Though the hotel is too small to have a pool or spa, it does have a good restaurant and a super terrace for watching the shiny yachts pass by.

The boutique **Hotel Park** (Hvar Town, tel. 021/718-337, www.hotelparkhvar.com, 1,773Kn d., including breakfast) opened in 2007. The 14 airy apartments and one room have pretty sea views, Internet, and plasma televisions.

The ◧ **Adriana Hotel** (Fabrika bb, tel. 021/750-200, www.suncanihvar.com, 2,837Kn d., including breakfast) is currently the only Croatian hotel included in the venerable Leading Small Hotels of the World. For the not-so-budget price you get a location overlooking the marina and the old city center, with indoor and outdoor pools, a spa, and a swank rooftop lounge. In 2008 the Sunčani Hvar chain (which runs the Adriana) unveiled their latest luxe hotel, the **Amfora Grand Beach Resort** (Majerovica bb, tel. 021/750-300, www.suncanihvar.com, 2,269Kn d.,

Hvar Town, a quiet fishing village most of the year – and anything but quiet in peak season

including breakfast), with a cascading pool, private 1930s stone cabanas for relaxing, and light, sleek rooms.

FOOD

A good value on the ever-pricier island of Hvar, **Luna** (Petra Hektorovića, tel. 021/741-400, noon–midnight daily in summer, noon–3 P.M. and 6 P.M.–midnight April and Sept., 85Kn) serves up dishes such as seafood pasta and meat with dumplings and mushroom sauce in the cheery dining room or on the superb rooftop terrace.

In Groda, **Macondo** (Petra Hektorovića, Groda, tel. 021/742-850, noon–2 P.M. and 6:30 P.M.–midnight Mon.–Sat., 6:30 P.M.–midnight Sun., closed Nov.–Mar., 130Kn) packs in tourists in season, making getting a table a bit of a challenge. The reason for the cozy place's popularity? The fresh daily catches served, as well as the great selection of cakes and desserts for dine-in or takeout.

The nearby **Konobo Menego** (Petra Hektorovića, Groda, tel. 021/742-036, www.menego.hr, 11:30 A.M.–2 P.M. and 5 P.M.–midnight daily, closed Dec.–Mar., 120Kn) has a traditional interior and a slightly out-of-the-box menu. Serving up tapa-size portions of local dishes, this restaurant has a big following. One of Hvar's trendier restaurants, **Yakša** (Petra Hektorovića, Groda, tel. 021/717-202, www.yaksahvar.com, 10 A.M.–4 P.M. and 7 P.M.–1 A.M. daily in summer, noon–2 P.M. and 7 P.M.–1 A.M. daily in winter, closed Dec.–Jan., 150Kn) is only 20 meters from the cathedral and serves up brunch (from omelets to American pancakes) and lunch and dinner (starters like young cheese over baked eggplants on tomato-lentil confit and mains like lobster and fries or honey chicken breast with green chile *sambal*). The ambience is nice too—in a cozy underground Gothic space with minimalist furniture or on an open-air patio. The restaurant also plans to offer accommodation in the near future.

On the less-touristed route, **Restoran Luviji** (tel. 021/741-646, 10 A.M.–2 P.M. and 7 P.M.–midnight daily, closed Oct.–May, 85Kn) serves the usual fish alongside out-of-this-world bread and some very good homemade wines, cultivated on Hvar and the Pakleni Islands.

If you'd like to dine away from Hvar's busiest

sections, head to **Zorače** (Uvala Zorače, tel. 021/745-638, 11 A.M.–11 P.M. daily in summer), six kilometers away on a quiet stretch of beach. The menu is predictable, the decor traditional, and the view from the cliff-top terrace completely out of this world. Another option is the out-of-the-fray **Robinson** (Mekičevića Bay, tel. 091/383-5160, www.robinson-hvar.hr, 11 A.M.–sunset daily June–Sept., no credit cards, 85Kn), an hour's walk from Hvar Town. There's no water, and no electricity, but plenty of local, organic food and grilled seafood, plus a nice bay where you can take a dip before or after lunch.

Two kilometers southeast of Hvar Town is Milna Bay, with lovely beaches and the totally unpretentious **Kamanjo's** (Uvala Milna hvarska, tel. 021/745-010, noon–midnight in summer, call for winter hours, 100Kn). The owners' philosophy is that it is difficult to cook well for a large crowd, so he keeps things small. Make sure to try some of their homemade brandies (from chamomile, rose petals, oranges, and artichokes), the restaurant's signature pastas, and other Italian-influenced dishes like beef risotto with saffron.

INFORMATION AND SERVICES

The Hvar Town **tourist office** (Trg sv Stjepana bb, tel. 021/741-059, www.tzhvar.hr, 8 A.M.–1 P.M. and 5–9 P.M. Mon.–Sat. and 9 A.M.–noon Sun. June–Sept., 8 A.M.–2 P.M. Mon.–Sat. Oct.–May) is located on the corner of the Pjaca.

Palmižana

A short water taxi ride away from Hvar Town, the over-100-year-old **Pansion Meneghello** (Palmižana, Sv. Klement, Pakleni Islands, tel. 021/717-270, www.palmizana.hr, closed Nov.–Mar., 461Kn d.) on Palmižana is like a vacation within a vacation. The quiet island is worlds away from the constant buzz of nearby Hvar and the gorgeous rooms and suites, decorated with a mix of antiques, modern art, and well-placed pops of color, have a style best defined as peaceful, laid-back luxe. The family-run hotel hosts special events during the summer, often involving themed art exhibitions. If you don't want to stay overnight, you can still come for lunch and a swim.

Stari Grad

Stari Grad is the point of entry for many ferries coming from Split, but there's plenty to see in this town that gets a lot less tourist traffic than the island's capital. It's also home to a growing art scene. Aficionados will enjoy cruising the narrow alleys looking for galleries and artists during the summer months. The most popular sight in Stari Grad is the **Tvrdalj** (tel. 021/765-068, 10 A.M.–1 P.M. and 6–8 P.M. daily June–Sept., 10Kn), the summer home of Hvar's 16th-century poet Petar Hektorović. Though the home is largely unimpressive, bits of the preserved gardens, a pretty fish pond, and dozens of inscriptions on the walls—all the work of Hektorović—make for a restful, contemplative meander. There's a 15th-century Dominican monastery nearby with a small **museum** (10 A.M.–noon and 4–7:30 P.M. Mon.–Sat. in summer, 10Kn) where you'll find some Greek tombstones, Hektorović artifacts, and a Tintoretto.

There are plenty of beaches in Stari Grad, though the best ones are on the southern side of the Riva towards Borić.

The Stari Grad **tourist office** (Nova Riva 2, tel. 021/765-763, www.stari-grad-faros.hr, 8 A.M.–9 P.M. daily June–Sept., 8 A.M.–2 P.M. Mon.–Fri. Oct.–May) can help hook you up with private accommodation, generally a much better option than the overpriced concrete resorts in the area. When you need to grab a bite, Stari Grad has two excellent options. The first, **Antika Restaurant and Café Bar** (Donja Kola, tel. 021/765-479, noon–3 P.M. and 6 P.M.–1 A.M. daily, closed Dec.–Jan., 80Kn), located in a 16th-century building, is a funky little spot with a very different menu from most small-town Dalmatian establishments. Try the steak with green pepper sauce. In the heart of the old town, ◖ **Jurin Podrum** (Donja kola 8, tel. 021/765-804, noon–2:30 P.M. and 6 P.M.–midnight daily in summer, 110Kn) has been famous with

Europe's elite since it opened in the 1930s (Edward VIII and Wallace Simpson dined here the year of his abdication). The restaurant offers dishes from a simple starter of new goat cheese topped with grilled vegetables to an unexpected spaghetti with octopus and zucchini, a featured dish on the menu.

Jelsa

Though Jelsa sees more and more tourists every year, it's nothing like Hvar Town. Take an hour or so to wander the old alleyways, admiring the stone buildings and the 16th-century **Crkva svetog Ivana** (Church of St. John). Though the beaches in Jelsa tend to get a bit crowded, the local **Mina** beach, next to the Hotel Mina, is good for kids. Just 1.5 kilometers away you'll find **Grebišce beach** with a small bar and restaurant, or take a water taxi from the Jelsa harbor to nudist **Zečevo** island or the usually not nudist **Glavica Peninsula.**

The **Hvar Hostel** (Jelsa bb, tel. 098/978-4143, www.hvar-hostel.com, 285Kn d.), formerly Pension Huljić, has much nicer rooms than you'd expect, plus a peaceful garden and a location that's walking distance to practically everything you need (beach, bus station, and restaurants, to name a few). A charming little family-run hotel conveniently located near the bus station, the **Pansion Murvica** (Sv Roko, Jelsa, tel. 021/761-405, www.murvica.net, no credit cards, 350Kn d., including breakfast) offers clean rooms and a good restaurant. **Huljić** (Banski Dolac, tel. 021/761-409, noon–3 p.m. and 7 p.m.–midnight daily, closed late Oct.–mid-April, no credit cards, 95Kn) serves plenty of dishes that are a departure from the ever-present grilled fish, plus tastings of the owners' own red and white wines. Eight kilometers southeast from town, (**Humac** (Humac, tel. 091/523-9463, noon–10 p.m. daily in summer, no credit cards, 90Kn) is a restaurant in a practically deserted village. All the dishes are cooked on the fire—there's no electricity in town—and romantic candlelight is provided.

If you're looking for something a bit more hopping, head to **Chuara** (Riva, tel. 091/575-5114, www.chuara-jelsa.hr, 9 a.m.–1 p.m. and 5 p.m.–5 a.m. daily in summer), for swish cocktails and DJ tunes.

Jelsa has a **tourist office** (Riva bb, tel. 021/761-918, www.tzjelsa.hr).

Sveta Nedelja

On the southern side of the island, almost due south of Stari Grad (though it's better connected to Jelsa), is the village of Sveta Nedelja, a must for wine lovers. You can overnight at the basic **Vila Irming** (Sveta Nedelja, tel. 021/745-768, www.irming.hr, closed Nov.–Apr., no credit cards, 425Kn d.) in the fishing village of Sveta Nedelja. It's not a fancy sort of place but there are nice beaches (paved and pebbled) a short walk away and you can take a water taxi pretty much anywhere on the island from the local marina (ask the staff to help you arrange transport).

As for wineries, be sure to hit up **Zlatan Plenković** (Sveta Nedelja, tel. 021/745-725, www.zlatanotok.hr, call for information about tours) and sample some of his Grand Cru wine, made from Plavac Mali grapes. The Grand Cru is most similar to an excellent Barolo, but with its own flair. He also has a guesthouse where you can stay and a restaurant, **Bilo Idro** (Sveta Nedelja, tel. 021/745-725, www.zlatanotok.hr, 9 a.m.–1 a.m. daily mid-May–mid-Oct.), which serves his wines plus great seafood in a waterfront location.

Svirče

A worthwhile excursion from either Jelsa or Vrboska, this small interior village is not only a way to get off the beaten path, but is also home to the **Tomić** (tel. 021/768-160, www.bastijana.hr, contact for hours and visits) winery. They produce a variety of wines and brandies, but it's most famous for its dessert *prosecco* called Hectorovich, after Hvar's most famous poet.

Vrboska

Vrboska is a quiet little town and a great location for beachgoers. The village has two interesting churches: the **Crkva svete Marije** (St. Mary's Church, 10 a.m.–noon and 6–7 p.m. Mon.–Sat., free), whose floor is largely made up of tombstones, and the Baroque **Crkva svetog**

Lovre (St. Lawrence's Church, 10 A.M.–noon Mon.–Sat., free) with a couple of pretty Italian paintings inside.

The most popular beach is **Glavica**, about one kilometer from Vrboska. If you have a car you can park at the Soline parking lot. **Soline** is the main beach here, drawing sun worshippers from many parts of the island. Walking 5–15 minutes from the parking lot to the north, you'll hit the nudist beaches, with big flat rocks perfect for roasting in your birthday suit, or continue to the romantic coves of Maslinica and Palinica.

Right in Vrboska, family-run **Villa Darinka** (tel. 021/774-188, no email or website, closed Nov.–Mar., 355Kn d.) has comfortable rooms with sea-facing balconies and neat-as-a-pin decor. For sustenance, try the **Restoran Gardelin** (tel. 021/774-280, www.gmp-artstudio.com/Gardelin, daily in summer, call for exact hours, 85Kn) for grilled fish, stewed fish, and baked fish.

Sućuraj

On the far eastern side of the island, the fishing village of Sućuraj is one of Hvar's quieter towns. A great place for beach lovers, the town is surrounded by lounging options. A short walk from the center of town you'll find sandy Cesminica to the south or pebbly Bilina to the north. You can rent a boat or hop in a water taxi from the small harbor to the sandy bays of Mlaska (north) or Perna (south).

Getting There and Around

Stari Grad is the main port serving ferries from Split (around 7 daily in the high season, 1.5 hours), Rijeka (13 hours, stops in Split), and Dubrovnik (7.5 hours, stops in Korčula). You can link to Makarska via the ferry at Sućuraj (only viable if you have your own car on the ferry, since there are no buses to speak of out of the small village).

If you're traveling without a car, the best way to get to town is the hydrofoil from Split (Jadrolinija, tel. 021/631-357, www.jadrolinija.hr), which takes less than an hour into Hvar Town, the center of all the action. There's also a catamaran (at least one daily in summer) linking Brač (from Bol) to the town of Jelsa on Hvar.

Buses are waiting for the larger ferries and link Hvar Town and Stari Grad (30 minutes). Buses from Stari Grad also connect with Vrboska and Jelsa (each 30 minutes). Keep in mind that buses on the island can be highly unpredictable.

You can rent mopeds and cars from Luka Rent (on Hvar Town's harbor, tel. 021/742-946) or Pelegrini Tours (Riva bb, Hvar Town, tel. 021/742-250, www.pelegrini-hvar.hr). Mopeds cost around 300Kn per day. The agencies are also good sources for boat and bicycle rentals.

VIS

A military base under Tito for some 40 years, Vis is a relatively new addition to the Croatian tourist trade. The island has long been filled with farmers and fishermen, who both know a thing or two about good food, making Vis somewhat of an unassuming gourmet destination. Though you'll still find your share of tourists in July and August, it's much quieter than many of the surrounding islands and coastline.

Vis Town

Located on the northeast side of Vis, Vis Town is the largest village on the island. Though it's popular with yachters—the main marina is located here—its history is more agricultural, with much of the produce and wines grown in the hills outside of town having supplied trade for the little port. These days you'll find top-quality restaurants and a handful of fun bars with a seafaring edge.

SIGHTS

There's not too much to see here, but the **Arheološki muzej** (Archaeological Museum, tel. 021/711-729, 10 A.M.–1 P.M. and 5–8 P.M. Tues.–Sun. in summer, 20Kn), located in the **Baterija**, an old Austrian fortress, has a nice collection of objects from Vis's Greek past. In Kut, the yachting section of town, the old patrician palaces, **Crkva svetog Ciprijana** (St. Cyprian's church), and a **British naval cemetery** are located in Vis's first (circa 1911) hotel, serves lunch and dinner as well. Tuck into French toast with syrup, pancakes with fresh oranges and lemon jam, or a bowl of orange soup for brunch, washed down with a strong cup of espresso.

The artsy **Kantun** (Biskupa Mihe Pusića 17, tel. 021/711-306, 6 P.M.–midnight daily, no credit cards, 90Kn) mixes traditional and modern in the decor as well as the menu. It's a solid choice for dinner with a phenomenal smoked tuna carpaccio, a variety of well-prepared pasta dishes, and some good-quality meat and fish as well.

One of the few pizza places with a good wine list, **Karijola** (Šetalište Viskog Boja 4, tel. 021/711-433, noon–late night daily July–Aug., 5–11 P.M. June and Sept., 70Kn) serves up super oven-baked pizza on a terrace with a pretty view.

Vila Kapiola (V. Nazora 32, tel. 021/711-755, 5 P.M.–midnight daily in season, reservations recommended, 110Kn) is one of Vis's best, nestled in a secret garden beside an old Italian villa under the shade of palm trees. The menu is local and the quality superb, with dishes like smoked fish soup and a selection of great local wines. **Pojoda** (Don Cvjetka Marasovića 8, tel. 021/711-575, noon–3 P.M. and 5 P.M.–midnight in summer, 4–11 P.M. in winter, 120Kn) is one of Croatia's most famous fish restaurants. Located in an old house complete with cloistered garden, the restaurant is beautiful—but the creations of

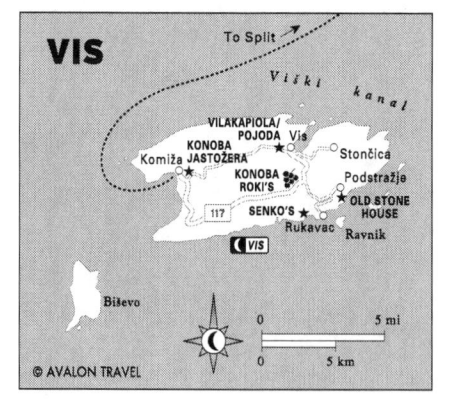

the main attractions. The cemetery is about a 20-minute walk from Kut, but just beyond it you'll find a wonderful gem of a beach at **Grandovac**. A 20-minute walk northwest of Vis Town's ferry landing you'll find a few crumbling graves at the **Helenističko groblje** (Ancient Greek Cemetery, afternoons daily in summer, free) and what's left of a few old Roman baths with some attractive mosaics.

ACCOMMODATIONS

Hotel Paula (Petra Hektorovića 2, tel. 021/711-362, www.hotelpaula.com, 690Kn d.) is a 35-room hotel in Kut, within Vis's old section. The stone building, with a peaceful courtyard and a good fish restaurant, houses simple but comfortable rooms with air-conditioning and satellite television.

You could also look into booking a room or apartment through one of the agencies in town. Try **Navigator** (Šetalište stare Isse 1, tel. 021/717-786, www.navigator.hr), which also rents cars and scooters.

FOOD

You can certainly eat well—very well, in fact—in Vis Town, though if you're looking for the absolute best, you'll need to check out other villages around the island. An excellent place to start your day is **Doručak kod Tihane** (Obala Sv. Jurja 5, tel. 021/718-472, www.restorantihana.com, 9 A.M.–1 P.M. and 6 P.M.–midnight daily, 70Kn), though the charming restaurant,

HIKING SAFELY ON VIS

Though there wasn't a war on Vis, there are potential land mines left over from the old military base. If you're going to hike, make sure to follow the rules. Watch for signs with a skull and/or crossbones that say *Pazi Mina*. It's also not a bad idea to check with the tourist office in Vis Town before doing any hiking or trekking in the wilderness.

the fishing village Komiža, on the western end of Vis

chef-owner Zoran Brajčić are the star attractions. Brajčić infuses the native Dalmatian cuisine with his Slavonian roots; dishes like the *manistra na brudet,* a bean and pasta soup, and the grilled belted bonito, treated to a spice rub and weighted down for 10 hours before cooking, provide diners with a stunning gourmet performance. *Hib,* a traditional biscuit made from ground dried figs, is a sweet ending to the evening.

INFORMATION AND SERVICES

Vis's **tourist office** (Šetalište stare Isse 5, tel. 021/717-017, www.tz-vis.hr, 9 A.M.–1 P.M. and 6–9 P.M. Mon.–Sat. in summer, 9 A.M.–1 P.M. Mon.–Fri. in winter) can help with maps, brochures, and information on hiking in the area.

Komiža

On the western end of Vis, ten kilometers from Vis Town, Komiža is a fishing village extraordinaire, slightly stubbly, laid-back, rather quiet, and washed with sun, much like many of the older fishermen in town. You'll find the 13th-century Venetian **Kaštel** (Castle Fort) by the sea, where the **Ribarski muzej** (Fishing Museum, 9 A.M.–noon and 6–10 P.M. daily, 10Kn) will help you get more in touch with the local culture and historical livelihood. There are great views from the Kaštel's 16th-century tower as well.

The most interesting of the town's churches is the **Gospa Gusarica** (Our Lady of the Pirates) near the Biševo Hotel, so named for the legend that claims a painting of the Virgin stolen by pirates made its way back to shore after a shipwreck.

Once a lobster storage facility, **Konoba Jastožera** (Gundulićeva 6, tel. 021/713-859, www.jastozera.com, 5 P.M.–midnight daily, closed late Oct.–mid-Apr., 300Kn) still wrestles fresh lobster out of an underwater cage for your dinner. Tables are placed on planks above the water and the sound of the sea lapping below is a great accompaniment to the food, which has been enjoyed by a number of celebrities (their photos line the walls). Lobster is the feature of the menu—lobster spaghetti, lobster cream soup, and several preparations of main-course lobster. Shrimp, mussels, and a smattering of meat dishes round out the offerings.

The simple and beautiful apartments at **Villa Nonna** (Ribarska 50, tel. 098/380-046, www.villa-nonna.com, no credit cards, 496Kn d.) are an excellent value—pleasingly furnished and only a minute's walk to the marina. If rooms here are booked ask the owners for recommendations around town.

Approximately half a dozen buses connect Komiža and Vis Town daily, taking about 25 minutes.

Stončića

Rent a boat or take a water taxi to Stončića, about six kilometers from Vis Town. The beaches in this sandy bay are heavenly and there's a lighthouse and a restaurant. Set in a romantic cove, **Stončica** (Stončica 1, tel. 021/711-669, lists summer hours as "always" and winter hours "by agreement," 100Kn) is a family restaurant serving their own homegrown and daily-catch specialties. The menu varies according to what's fresh, but you'll always find grilled fish and vegetables. Dive into the *pašticada nona* when available and sample the homemade spicy lamb salami *(kulen)* and dark red prosecco while sitting under the shade of palm trees and meandering vines.

Though **Senko's** (Mola trovna, tel. 098/352-5803, noon–midnight daily, no credit cards, 110Kn) is no longer undiscovered, it's still an experience. Located in a cove on the southern side of Vis, between Stončica and Stupišće, is chef-owner Senko Karuza's laid-back restaurant, filled with wooden tables and benches on a stone terrace overlooking the water. The fruits and vegetables come from Senko's organic garden. The menu is whatever's available and whatever he feels like making, and all of it is good, from smoked fish soup with rosemary and smoked eel soup to fish or bean and pasta stew to grilled fish and shrimp, flavored with wild herbs and washed down with some of Senko's wine. It's a must to make a reservation in season.

Rukavac and Biševo

In Rukavac village, 10 kilometers south of Vis Town on the southern side of the island, you'll find **Srebrena plaža** (Silver Beach), another piece of paradise just across from the islet of **Biševo,** home to the legendary **Modra špilja** (Blue Cave, 30Kn), reached only from the sea. The only way to describe the grotto is as an other-worldly mix of bright blue that seems like it's lit from below, covered by a canopy of dark rock. However you see it, it's been a major tourist attraction since the 1880s. If you'd like to visit the cave, take a trip from either the Komiža or Vis Town harbors (the excursions are heavily advertised) or take a taxi boat.

Natural Holiday (Salbunara Bay, tel. 098/173-1673, www.bisevo.org, no credit cards, approximately 3,350Kn weekly depending on requested excursions and meals) is part hotel, part lifestyle concept. It's a totally green village of huts powered along by solar panels and the wind, with mosquito netting and ergonomic beds. It's not luxurious, but it is peaceful. Lay back in one of their hammocks while waiting on dinner, prepared by the owners, of organic vegetables and fresh fish.

You'll need to book early to snatch one of the rooms at **Old Stone House** (Rukavac, tel. 098/131-4179 or 44-1834/814-533 (UK), www.weareactive.com, 5,950Kn per week includes activities, daily breakfast, four lunches, and three dinners) in the miniscule village of Rukavac. The home is super stylish and best of all includes an invigorating customized activity program that can consist of mountain biking, kayaking, hiking, and a spot of yoga.

Rukavac is easily reached from Vis Town on a good asphalt road. You can also take a taxi boat.

Wineries

Eleven kilometers east of Komiža or seven kilometers south of Vis Town, **Konoba Roki's** (Plisko Polje 17, tel. 021/714-004, noon–late daily April–Oct., no credit cards, 120Kn) is a winery and restaurant a short drive from Vis Town by cab or car (the restaurant will pick up parties of four or more from Vis Town). Not only is the food good but it's fun to sample the red and white wines produced by the owners.

Getting There and Around
Vis is served by at least one daily car ferry from Split year-round (2 hours 20 minutes, 45Kn). In the summer, there are one or two more catamarans from Split (1 hour 15 minutes, 60Kn).

Komiža is connected with Vis Town by a bus that runs according to ferry schedules. In the summer it's quite reliable, but out of the high season you may need to wait (bring a book).

To get around the island, it's not a bad idea to rent a small car or scooter. Agencies such as Navigator (Šetalište stare Isse 1, tel. 021/717-786, www.navigator.hr) and Ionios (Obala Svetog Jurja 36, tel. 021/711-532) rent transportation options around the island—Navigator offers cars and scooters, and Ionios offers scooters and bicycles.

Korčula Harbor

KORČULA
Korčula, a small island with a much grander past, is filled with small museums, pretty festivals, and tiny sun-washed villages. There are plenty of pebbly beaches lapped by the calm Adriatic waters and the island is home to some quality white wines and top olive oils, famous for their rich flavor, from the town of Vela Luka. Korčula was settled by the Greeks in the 6th century B.C., when it was known as Black Corfu. The island was relatively unimportant until the Venetians came in the 10th century, using it as an important naval base. Korčula thrived from the 13th to the 15th centuries, though an outbreak of plague in 1571 brought an end to the island's importance. Korčula began to find life again as a tourist destination in the 1920s and by the 1970s the island was burgeoning with hotels and restaurants to serve the summer visitors.

One of the highlights of Korčula is its colorful **festivals.** The Moreška sword dancers that perform throughout the summer for visitors, the processions held during Easter week, and the reenactment of the 1298 Battle Korčula (early Sept.) all lend a bit of local flavor to a stay on the island. Contact the Korčula **tourist office** (Obala Franje Tuđmana, tel. 020/715-701, www.korcula.net, 8 A.M.–3 P.M. and 4–10 P.M. Mon.–Sat. and 8 A.M.–1:30 P.M. Sun. June–Oct., 8 A.M.–2 P.M. Mon.–Sat. Nov.–May) for more information on times and locations of events.

Korčula Town
Often compared with Dubrovnik, Korčula Town reminds visitors of a smaller version of the seaside walled city. But at a closer glance you'll find the Venetians, who built the small city, did a much better job of planning than the planners of Dubrovnik. Streets are laid out to make use of summer winds and to keep out the bitter northeasterly *bura*. Still, the Venetians seem to get lost in the limelight created by the town's most famous citizen, Marco Polo, likely (though not proven) born here in 1254. You'll see his name used in everything from pizzas to hotels to desserts.

SIGHTS
While the claim that Marco Polo was from Korčula is not unreasonable, the idea that the

circa-17th-century house touted as the **House of Marco Polo** (Ulica DePolo, 9 A.M.–9 P.M. daily in summer, 15Kn) was actually his house is a very big stretch. Plans have been underway for years now to turn the house into a museum, but you can still only climb to the top of the tower for some nice views over the water.

Heading south towards the small space known as the main square, called the **Trg Sv. Marka** or the **Pjaceta,** you'll find the **Gradski muzej** (Town Museum, Trg Sv. Marka bb, tel. 020/711-420, 10 A.M.–9 P.M. Mon.–Sat. in summer, call for winter hours, 15Kn), housed in a 16th-century Venetian palace. The star exhibits are a 4th-century Greek tablet, the earliest proof of civilization on the island, and a mock-up of a peasant kitchen.

Across from the museum is the **Katedrala svetog Marka** (St. Mark's Cathedral, Trg Sv. Marka bb, tel. 020/711-049, 9 A.M.–2 P.M. and 5–7 P.M. daily, April–Oct., 15Kn). The imposing building is considered one of the most beautiful Croatian churches. Inside, look for the two works by Tintoretto, particularly the restored 1550 painting of St. Mark between St. Bartholomew and St. Jerome, and the frothy stone canopy carved by local stonemason Marko Andrijić in the late 15th century. Next door you'll find the *riznica* (treasury, tel. 020/711-049, 9 A.M.–2 P.M. and 5–7 P.M. daily Apr.–Oct., call for winter hours, 15Kn), filled with a wonderful but modest art collection of Dalmatian and Italian Renaissance painters.

West of the old town, fans of more modern works will appreciate the **Galerija Maksimiljana Vanke** (Memorial Collection of Maksimiljan Vanka, Put Sv. Nikole, 9 A.M.–noon and 6–9 P.M. daily July–Aug., 5Kn), with paintings from art nouveau painter Maksimiljan Vanka as well as occasional exhibits by other Croatian artists.

ACCOMMODATIONS

A minute's walk from the ferry stop, rooms at **Roberta's Guesthouse** (Put Sv. Nikole 24, tel. 020/711-247, robertamk@hotmail.com, 290Kn d., including breakfast) are cozy and the hostess, Roberta, is a delight. Try to book the room with the small waterfront balcony.

The **Royal Apartments** (Trg Petra Segedina 4, tel. 098/184-0444, open June–Oct., no credit cards, 690Kn d.) aren't fancy but they're clean, the owner is very kind and helpful, and the location (slightly west of the old town on a small waterfront square) is wonderful. The renovated **Hotel Marko Polo** (Šetalište Frana Kršinića, tel. 020/726-100, www.htp-korcula.hr, 965Kn d., including breakfast) has sleek and trendy though incredibly small rooms. The hotel has indoor and outdoor pools and access to a pebbly beach about one kilometer from the bus station. Though the property has received an overhaul, unfortunately the service has not. Opening in spring 2009, the **Lesić Dimitri Palace** (Don Pavla Poše 1-6, tel. 020/715-560, www.lesic-dimitri.com) promises to be the gem of Korčula

FOOD

The island offers a plethora of seafood restaurants, but the pastry shop **Cukarin** (Hrvatske bratske zajednice bb, tel. 020/711-055, 8:30 A.M.–noon and 6–9 P.M. daily) is the island's true culinary gem. Make sure to try the Marko Polo *bombica,* a chocolate-encased cream delight, or the walnut-filled *klašun,* and take home a bottle of one of the dessert wines made from the local *grk* grape. Dine alfresco on the square next to the Town Hall at **Gradski Podrum** (Trg Antuna Kaporova, tel. 020/711-222, 11 A.M.–2 P.M. and 6–10:30 P.M. daily, closed Nov.–Mar., 85Kn). The menu offers something for everyone, from pasta and salads to meat and fish. Even though **Kanavelić** (Ulica Franje Tuđmana 1904, tel. 020/711-800, 6 P.M.–1 A.M. daily, closed Dec.–Apr., 90Kn) is popular with the tourist trade, it has a nice ambience (high ceilings, a courtyard with fruit trees) and the food is good, particularly the fish stew served over a steaming mound of polenta. The outdoor terraces of the rustic **Konoba Belin** (Zrnovo Prvo Selo, tel. 091/503-9258, www.konobabelin.com, 10 A.M.–midnight daily in season, no credit cards, 100Kn), some two kilometers away from town in Zrnovo Prvo Selo (First Village Zrnovo), are the best part of the busy restaurant. The food is solid, too, with wind-cured ham and cheese appetizers, seafood risotto, and grilled fish.

Adio Mare (Sv. Roka 2, tel. 020/711-253, 5 P.M.–midnight daily in summer, call for winter hours, 135Kn) is a staple on the Korčula restaurant scene and generally declared one of the island's best. It's imperative to book a dinner reservation in season to snag a table at this seafood restaurant just steps from the main square.

Call in advance to order *peka* at **Ranč Maha** (Zrnovo–Pupnat Road, tel. 098/494-389, 1–11 P.M. daily in summer, call for hours in winter, no credit cards, 95Kn), a family farm in the hills above town where hikers and tourists converge to eat the clay oven–baked meat and seafood washed down with some seriously strong homemade herbal grappa. In winter a crackling fire makes dining here even better.

Lumbarda

The village of Lumbarda, six kilometers from Korčula Town, is best known for its sandy beaches. A short drive south of the village will bring you to Sveti Križ (Holy Cross Church) set amongst vineyards, where you'll veer left to **Bilin Zal,** a fairly quiet beach with rocky sections. For lunch there's a good little *konoba* here in the ruins of an old summer residence. Keep driving southeast to reach **Vela Pržina,** facing the Italian coast, about 15 minutes away. Pržina is a long beach, but quite popular as well, and gets filled early.

If you don't mind sharing the garden with the occasional goat, stay at the farmhouse **Pansion Marinka** (Lumbarda, tel. 098/344-712, marinka.milina-bire@du.htnet.hr, www.korcula.net/firme/private/lumbarda/bire_marinka.htm, no credit cards, 230Kn d., including breakfast), a grandmotherly bed-and-breakfast with kind owners who are happy to regale you with stories of the island if you ask. The rooms are basic but cozy and sampling some of the farm's products, particularly the olive oil, is a real treat. One and a half kilometers from Lumbarda the **Apartments Val** (Uvala Račišće bb, tel. 020/712-430, www.korcula-val.com, 290Kn d.) are situated on a quiet bay. Each apartment has a sea-facing terrace and satellite TV and the hosts can rent bicycles and a small boat for cruising around the island. The casual, quiet restaurant **More** (Lumbarda, tel. 020/712-068, lunch and dinner daily in summer, call for hours in winter, 110Kn) has a shady vine-enveloped terrace. The specialty of the chef is the melt-in-your-mouth lobster accompanied by pasta in tomato sauce.

Vela Luka

A 20-minute walk from town is the **Vela Špila cave** (tel. 020/813-602, www.vela-spila.hr, hours vary, 10Kn), a limestone cave inhabited by various people since 18,000 B.C. Archaeological finds from the site can be found in Vela Luka's small **Gradski muzej** (Town Museum, ask at tourist office for hours, 10Kn). The **tourist office** in town (Ulica 41 br. 11, tel. 021/813-619, www.tzvelaluka.hr, 8 A.M.–9 P.M. Mon.–Sat. June–Sept., 8 A.M.–3 P.M. Mon.–Sat. winter) can direct you to private rooms, good restaurants, and where to buy some of the town's famous olive oils. You'll find two small islands just off the coast of Vela Luka. Taxi boats can take you to **Proizd** (20 minutes, 35Kn) or **Ošjak** (30 minutes, 60Kn), where pretty pebbly beaches and small restaurants are the perfect spot to get away—don't be shocked by the nudists.

Getting There and Around

The island's two major ferry ports (Korčula Town and Vela Luka) have good connections to the mainland. Jadrolinija (www.jadrolinija.hr) runs the majority of the ferries, with a daily car ferry (in summer, check with Jadrolinija for winter connections) connecting both ports with Split (around 3 hours, 50Kn), often making a stop in Hvar as well. There's also a ferry connecting Korčula Town with Dubrovnik (3 hours). Catamarans link Dubrovnik and Korčula Town (4 weekly, 2.5 hours) as well as Split (daily, 2.25 hours). Both trips cost around 60Kn.

Korčula has excellent connections with the Pelješac Peninsula, with connections from Orebić on the mainland and Korčula Town in only 15 minutes. There's at least one daily car ferry and one passenger ferry on summer weekdays.

Buses regularly connect Korčula Town with Lumbarda and Vela Luka (6 on weekdays, less weekends, 1 hour, 35Kn). Water taxis are another good way to jump between Korčula Town and Lumbarda.

There's a daily bus to Dubrovnik (twice daily in summer, once daily in winter, 3 hours, 95Kn), but since it often fills up in summer it's a good idea to make a reservation in advance.

SKOJI ISLANDS

To really get away, rent a small boat on Korčula (you can try Rent a Djir, Obala Hrvatskih mornara, tel. 020/711-908, www.korcula-rent.com, which also rents cars and scooters) and navigate your way to the Skoji Islands, a group of 19 small islands just off the coast of Lumbarda. The two largest islands, Badija and Vrnik, have places for a light lunch as well as beaches. The other, uninhabited islands are just the place to find your own stretch of pebbly perfection.

LASTOVO

The island of Lastovo was chosen by settlers as a safe harbor from the constant raids of Uskok, Turkish, and Genoese pirates. Built in the crater of a former volcano, the town is almost invisible from the tall cliffs that surround it. In 2006, the island was declared a national park and it's a great place to see Dalmatia as it once was. It's served by only one ferry from Split a day, and the narrow alleyways of the old village are relatively uncrowded, especially out of high season. In between chilling out, you can visit the 15th-century **Crkva svetog Kuzme i Damjana** (Church of Sts. Cosmos and Damian) or hike up to the 19th-century fort for some stellar views, and then try to find a **water taxi** (ask at the tourist office or the marina) to take you to the small island of **Šaplun** for even more waterfront peace and quiet.

Festivals

The island of Lastovo is famous for its **Poklad festival,** a winter carnival centering around a giant effigy of a Turk (from the medieval era when the island suffered constant pressure from the invading Ottomans) that is carried around town and treated quite poorly before being lifted by rope above the town and burned. It's loud, it's a little strange (lots of drunken shouting involved), and it's totally interesting—one of those festivals completely unaware of any tourists who might have ventured to the island in winter to see it. As with Mardi Gras, the biggest celebration is on the Tuesday before Ash Wednesday. Contact the Lastovo **tourist office** (in Ubli on the main square, tel. 020/801-018, www.lastovo-tz.net, 8 A.M.–noon Mon.–Fri.) for more information.

Accommodations and Food

The **Vila Antica** (Sv. Kuzme i Damjana 3, tel. 098/447-311, www.vila-antica.com, 600Kn d.) in Lastovo village is a pretty old stone house, simply but tastefully outfitted, that's walking distance to the bus station, restaurants, and the beach, accessed via a shady path. The local diving center also runs a small hotel, the **Ladesta** (Uvala Pasadur, tel. 020/802-100, www.diving-paradise.net, 275Kn d.), near the port of Ubli. The circa-1837 **Struga Lighthouse** (Skrivena luka 110, tel. 01/245-2909, www.adriatica.net, 298Kn d.) has several simply furnished apartments run by the lighthouse keepers, who also cook filling meals for guests. From here you can explore Lastovo's villages and festivals.

If you ever wanted to live like Robinson Crusoe, **Mrčara Island** (tel. 021/384-279 or 099/212-0853, branko.pavelin@st.t-com.hr, www.adriatic-lastovo.vze.com, 922Kn d.), just off the coast of Lastovo, is the place to go. Six rooms in a stone house and three little cabins (a nice word for shacks) offer back-to-basics accommodation and facilities. Read: There's no electricity and washing and cooking are done with rainwater. In return you get some of the most beautiful nature and a fun, friendly atmosphere with like-minded guests.

The **Konoba Augusta Insula** (Zaklopatica Bay, tel. 020/801-167, www.augustainsula.com, 100Kn) serves up lobster spaghetti and a good white wine, made by the owners, on a waterfront terrace.

Getting There and Around

A daily car ferry connects the island with Split via Hvar Town and Vela Luka on Korčula. The ferry takes about three hours from Split (about 60Kn) and docks at the village of Ubli on Lastovo. Taxis wait here to ferry you to various spots around the island.

MLJET

There's not so much in terms of sights on Mljet besides the natural beauty of one of Dalmatia's most unspoiled islands. Just across from Dubrovnik, this heavily forested national park has a unique feature—two sparkling saltwater lakes. The largest lake has its own island, on which stands a 12th-century Benedictine monastery.

Sights and Recreation

The **Mljet National Park** is the biggest draw on Mljet, covering one third of the island. The crown jewels are the saltwater Veliko and Malo jezero (Big and Small Lake). Veliko jezero has a small island within the lake, topped by the Benedictine Svete Marije (St. Mary's), a church and 12th-century monastery. Other than that the biggest attractions of the island are sport and relaxation. **Biking** the island is the best way to get around (rent bikes from the Polače harbor, the Hotel Odisej, or the park's ticket office, all around 90Kn daily), though you can also rent a canoe or kayak (try Adriatic Kayak Tours, www.adriatickayaktours.com) or go windsurfing or diving (arranged through the Hotel Odisej). The **diving** is interesting since a 3rd-century Roman

---

LIGHTHOUSE ACCOMMODATIONS ON THE CROATIAN COAST

Some lighthouses on the Croatian coast are a bit out of the way, while others are totally remote, but all of them offer cheap, interesting accommodation on islands all over Croatia. One of the more famous lighthouses is on Palagruža, an island whose rocky shores are rumored to be the resting place of Greek hero Diomedes; the island's sunlit coves are fringed by the Adriatic's most startlingly blue waters. Many of the lighthouses are the ultimate in secluded escapes, with lots of flora and fauna to discover and abundant marine life, perfect for divers and snorkelers. It's imperative to bring your own provisions, though you may be able to arrange for meals or at least fresh fish from the lighthouse keeper. Check out **Adriatica.net** for more information and reservations for lighthouses on the coast.

shipwreck and a sunken WWII German torpedo boat are right off the coast.

Accommodations

At the mouth of Veliko Jezero, the **Srsen Apartments** (Soline bb, tel. 020/744-032, sandra.srsen@du.t-com.hr, 375Kn d.) have pretty water views and a large communal terrace. In the heart of Mljet National Park you'll find the beautiful (**Villa Jezero** (Njivice 2, tel. 020/744-019, www.jezero.tk, 496Kn d., including breakfast), a huge old limestone building that has served guests since 1934. The rooms are simple and the meals are lovingly prepared by the owners by arrangement. This is out-of-the-way peace at its best. To get there you'll take the national park bus to the owners' boat (ask when you get on the bus), which will take you across the lake; call to arrange pickup. It's plain, and it's a 1970s communist relic, but the **Hotel Odisej** (Pomena, tel. 020/744-022, www.hotelodisej.hr, 795Kn d., including breakfast) does meet basic requirements for shelter. Actually it's not all that bad. Some rooms have nice waterfront balconies and the staff is a pretty friendly bunch.

Food

(**Marijina Konoba** (Prožura, tel. 020/746-113, 8 A.M.–midnight in summer, call for winter hours, 95Kn) in Prožura is the definition of a family restaurant. The owners grow or catch everything on the menu, as well as prepare the food and serve the guests. Boats can be tied to the moorings in front. On the shaded terrace overlooking the bay the restaurant serves homemade cheese marinated in oil and brick oven–baked lobster with potatoes along with a selection of wines from their well-stocked cellar.

Though there are plenty of tourist-oriented restaurants preying on visitors to St. Mary's Island, **Melita** (St. Mary's Island, tel. 020/744-145, 10 A.M.–midnight daily, closed Oct.–Apr., no credit cards, 120Kn) is the real deal, located inside the monastery near the church. It's not cheap but the location is prime and the food is good. In Bavino Polje you'll find the bar **Komarac** (Sršenovići 44, no phone, 8:45 A.M.–midnight daily, no credit cards, 70Kn), a mosquito-themed bar with an eccentric vibe, perfect for a laid-back drink. Next door is **Triton** (Sršenovići 43, tel. 020/745-131, 10 A.M.–midnight daily, closed Nov.–Mar., no credit cards, 95Kn), an amiable place specializing in walnut liqueur and goat. If you're not a fan, they have seafood and other meats as well.

Getting There and Around

You can visit Mljet as a day trip from Dubrovnik, taking the passengers-only Nona Ana catamaran (Atlantagent, Obala Stjepana Radića 26, Dubrovnik, tel. 020/313-355, www.atlantagent.com, 70Kn) from Gruž in the morning, usually around 9 A.M. or 10 A.M. The boat stops at Sobra and Polače before heading back from Gruž in mid- to late afternoon. You'll have to stay overnight if you take the Jadrolinija car ferry, also departing from Gruž harbor, leaving in the afternoon and returning the following morning. It docks in Sobra, a 20-minute drive away from the national park.

Buses meet ferries in Sobra and connect to Polače and Pomena (both take over an hour), but they're not always reliable, particularly outside the busiest months of July and August. To get around and explore the island, it's really helpful to have a car. Mini Brum (tel. 020/745-260 or 098/285-566) rents cars from several locations on Mljet. Renting a bike is another option. Try the Polače harbor, the Hotel Odisej, or the park's ticket office, all charging around 90Kn daily.

NORTHERN DALMATIA

Northern Dalmatia does not have the blockbuster destinations of its southern counterpart, but its charming coastal towns are full of Roman-Veneto architecture and make great departure points for discovering private retreats and fishing excursions. It is a bit harder to find a good beach in this area, but they do exist, especially on some of the uninhabited islands just off the coast. The real standouts of Northern Dalmatia are Zadar, with lots of Roman relics and a culture all its own, and the Kornati Islands, a small wild archipelago with national park status. As for overlooked highlights, Šibenik's old town is a must-see that's also a good place to get out of the way of many of the summer's tourists. There's also tiny but lovely Trogir, full of fine well-preserved structures from the Middle Ages, though it fills to capacity with holidaying Europeans in the summer months, making it a bit harder to see the charm.

And cities aren't the only gems of the region. Natural beauty abounds in the area's national parks, in the karst landscape of Paklenica, the stunning Plitvice Lakes, the limestone cliffs of the Kornati, and the beautiful Krka, a rushing river punctuated by waterfalls. Though technically inland, the Plitvice Lakes, one of Croatia's busiest tourist destinations, make a great stop-off on your way to or from the coast or as a day trip from the Northern Dalmatian coastal towns.

Good food is not at all hard to find here, with dozens of seafood restaurants and places serving spit-roasted lamb, one dish with which the region holds lots of expertise.

© SHANN FOUNTAIN ČULO

HIGHLIGHTS

◖ **The Forum:** Zadar's Roman forum is the central attraction in a town filled with Roman ruins, loads of local culture, and a not-quite-discovered vibe. The giant square is littered with ancient columns and surrounded by worth-a-visit churches and museums (page 72).

◖ **Dugi Otok:** A great choice for beach bums, this island's Telašćica Bay nature park is filled with spots for swimming and sunning (page 80).

◖ **Donja Jezera in Plitvice Lakes National Park:** The pooling and cascading lakes in Plitvice are bordered by well-marked paths and lush forests. The Donja jezera, closest to the main entrance, are highlighted by the park's biggest waterfalls and are a must-see on the way to or from the coast (page 84).

◖ **Kornati Islands:** Made up of a string of scruffy islands, this national park is filled with wildlife, deserted stone houses, and a veritable flotilla of top-quality fish restaurants (page 85).

◖ **Katedrala svetog Jakova:** Juraj Dalmatinac's stunning cathedral overlooking the water in Šibenik is just the beginning of the often unnoticed town's sun-washed medieval core (page 88).

◖ **Krka National Park:** Whether you only scratch the surface by visiting the stepped rushing falls at Skradinski Buk or continue on to the park's fairy-tale Byzantine monastery, the beauty of the place makes it obvious why this is one of the region's most-visited destinations (page 92).

LOOK FOR ◖ TO FIND RECOMMENDED SIGHTS, ACTIVITIES, DINING, AND LODGING.

PLANNING YOUR TIME

If you have only two to three nights, try to fit in Zadar, a trip to the Kornati Islands, and perhaps a stop at Jurlinovi Dvori for a taste of traditional Dalmatia and at the famous restaurant Torcida near Šibenik for some *janjetina* (lamb)—this will give you a nice overview of the region. If you have another day or two, spend the night in Šibenik's old town, squeezing in a quick tour around town and a ferry to one of the islands just off the coast for a bit of relaxing. Trogir is close to Split, even closer to Split's airport, making it convenient to spend half a day in transit.

Not surprisingly, the coastal towns and islands are the busiest in July and August. Despite potential crowds around tourist attractions and shops in Zadar and Trogir, you won't find yourself overwhelmed on some of the off-the-coast islands, where you can keep walking until you get to a patch of undiscovered pebble shore. However, the best times to visit are May, June, and September, when the limestone is warm with the sun, but not so warm you're immediately running for the shade. The tourist numbers are dramatically lower in these months, though

NORTHERN DALMATIA 71

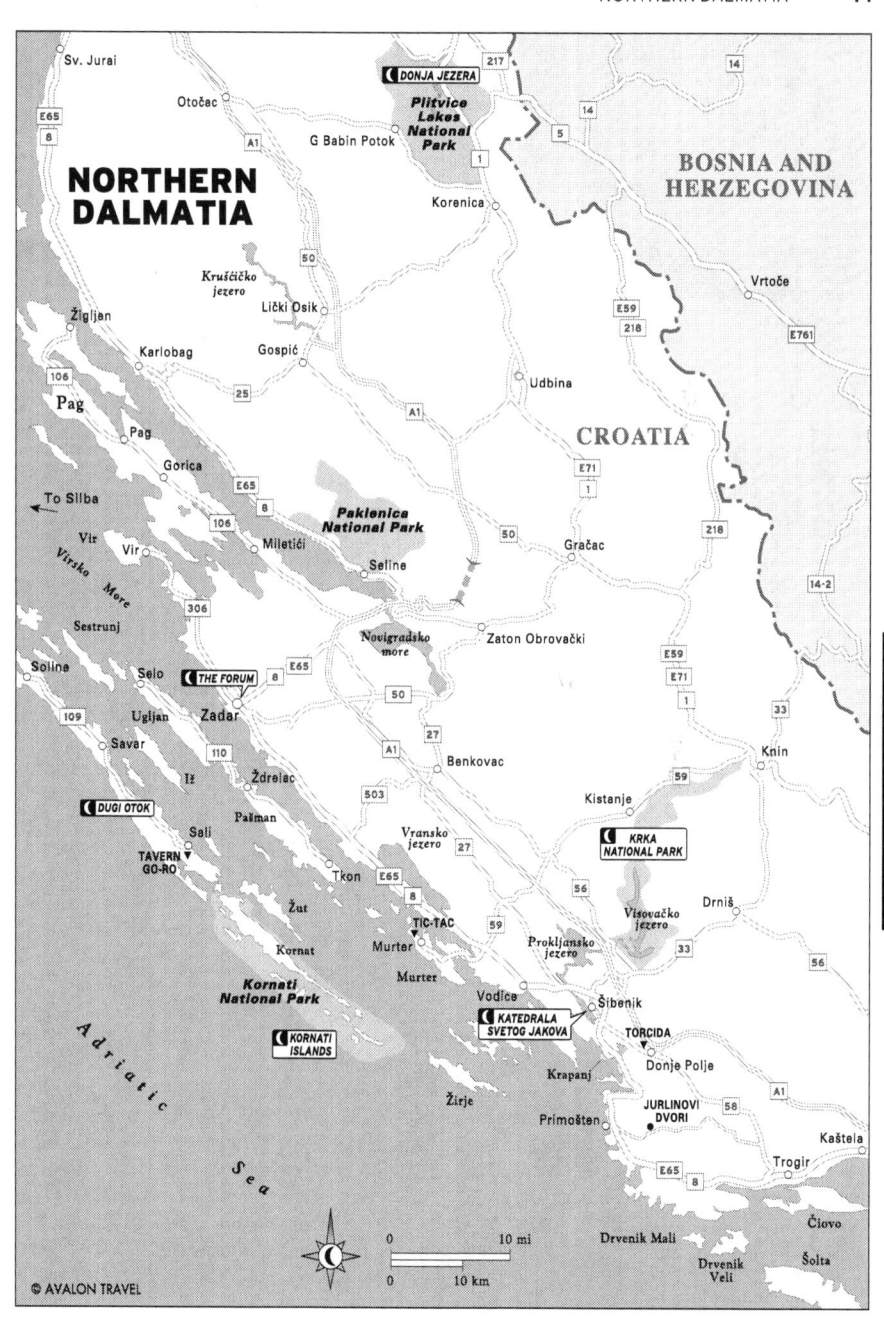

if you're planning to party, spring and fall aren't the time for it. Most of the fellow tourists during this time of year are in their retirement years.

Winter can be either an excellent time to visit (some days turn out sunny and warm enough for only a light coat) or an awful one (if the infamous *bura* is blowing). Some establishments, particularly on the islands, are closed during the winter months. However, it can be a nice time to come if you want to have the entire region to yourself.

Zadar

Zadar is one of Dalmatia's larger cities, though it never feels big. The town has real soul—likely derived from all the hardships it has faced over the years. It was bombed over 70 times by the Allies in World War II (reasons for which are still quite unclear) and held under siege during the Homeland War. Zadar has lots of architecture—from the Roman to Austro-Hungarian municipal buildings. The city is home to Croatia's oldest university, established by Dominican monks in 1396, making it quite a vibrant town when school is in session. When it's not, the number of students is replaced and tripled by tourists who pile in from the beach resorts nearby. Still, one has the feeling that the place is not quite discovered and it maintains its own vibe, independent of summering travelers.

HISTORY

Zadar (called Zara in Italian) was long under Venetian rule and the Italian influence in town has always been strong. The city was even given to Italy in 1921 before being returned to Croatia as a part of Tito's Yugoslavia in the late 1940s.

Damage from World War II was replaced with a crop of modern structures, giving the old town an organic feel as mid-century apartment blocks share a wall with Austro-Hungarian buildings, with discarded Roman columns not a block away. The city received even more damage when Serbian paramilitaries and the JNA (Yugoslav People's Army) surrounded the city in 1991, not completely retreating until 1995.

It has taken Zadar some time to recover economically from the siege. However, the fishing industries, the ferry port, and the appeal of the old-town core, with its museums and Roman architecture, are bringing kuna and tourists back in droves as Zadar once again becomes a destination for those in the know.

SIGHTS

◀ The Forum

Zadar's main square is referred to as the Forum, though it looks a bit more like a junkyard for old Roman columns (only one of the Forum's original columns remains standing). You'll find a lot of the pieces recycled inside the **Crkva svetog Donata** (St. Donat's Church, Zeleni trg, 9 A.M.–10 P.M. daily in summer, 10Kn), today only a tourist stop and musical venue (due to the excellent acoustics). Built at the beginning of the 9th century, the stark Byzantine church was built with remnants of columns, plaques, and other stone pieces the Romans left behind. In July and August the St. Donat Musical Evenings are held inside.

At the northern end of the Forum, steps away from St. Donat's Church, you'll find the **Katedrala svete Stošije** (Cathedral of St. Anastasia, Trg Sv. Stošije, 8 A.M.–6 P.M. daily in summer, 8 A.M.–12:30 P.M. daily in winter, free), a late Romanesque church from the 12th and 13th centuries that displays some magnificent stonework. The interior has some beautiful 13th-century frescoes as well as the 9th-century sarcophagus of St. Anastasia. For some super views of town you can climb up the 56-meter 19th-century **bell tower** (9 A.M.–8 P.M. daily in summer, 10Kn) built by English architect T. G. Jackson.

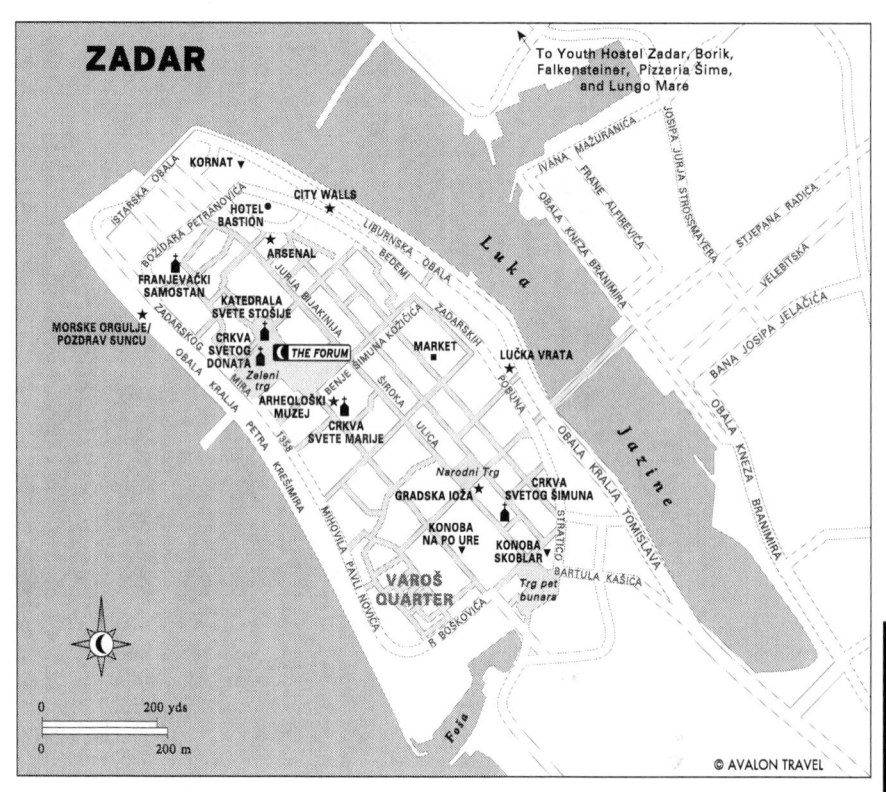

Trg Opatice Čike
Nun Čika Square

Across from St. Donat's Church, the Trg Opatice Čike connects to the southern side of the Forum. Here you'll find the **Arheološki muzej** (Archaeological Museum, Trg Opatice Čike 1, tel. 023/254-626, www.amzd.hr, 9 A.M.–2 P.M. and 5–9 P.M. daily Apr.–Sept., 9 A.M.–2 P.M. daily Oct.–Mar., 10Kn), whose plain building offers a stark modern contrast to the ancient relics around it. Inside, over 100,000 pieces from the prehistoric to the Romans to medieval times can be found on the museum's three floors, including a model of the Forum as it once was.

Next to the Arheološki muzej is the 11th-century **Crkva svete Marije** (St. Mary's Church, Trg Opatice Čike, tel. 023/250-496, 8 A.M.–noon and 5–8 P.M. daily, free) with a 16th-century facade, bombed during Allied raids on Zadar. The church is nice (and a mishmash of styles, from original recycled Roman columns to ornate Baroque balconies added in the 19th century), but the real finds are in the church's museum. the exhibit **Zlato i srebro Zadra** (Gold and Silver of Zadar, Trg Opatice Čike, tel. 023/250-496, 10 A.M.–12:30 P.M. and 6–7:30 P.M. Mon.–Fri. and 10 A.M.–noon Sat. in summer, call for winter hours, 20Kn) is treasure trove of sacral art, caskets, icons, and Byzantine crafts housed in the *samostan* (convent) next door to the church.

Franjevački samostan
Franciscan Monastery

Zadar's Franjevački samostan (Zadarskog mira, tel. 023/250-468, 7:30 A.M.–noon and 4:30–6 P.M. daily, free) is said to have been

Crkva svetog Donata, in Zadar's main square

founded by St. Francis in 1219. Thought to be the oldest Gothic church in Dalmatia, it has an interior that is mostly Renaissance. There's not much to see here beyond a few graves, though the well at the center of the courtyard garden is rather poignant given it was one of the few sources of drinking water for the city during the Homeland War of the early 1990s.

Morske orgulje
Sea Organ

Built in 2005, the Morske orgulje, located on the Obala kralja Petra Krešimira IV, is the inventive idea of local architect Nikola Bašić. The organ looks like a set of giant steps; the power of the waves forces interesting organic sounds out of the openings between the stairs. At night you can watch a stunning light show, **Pozdrav Suncu** (The Greeting to the Sun), also by Bašić, where a 22-meter circle soaks up sun in its solar panels during the day and starts to emit a glowing amalgam of colors at night.

City Walls

From the sea organ you can walk along the 16th-century city walls down the Liburnska obala to the southeastern **Lučka vrata** (Port Gate), fashioned from a Roman triumphal arch into a Renaissance grand entrance topped with the Lion of Venice. There's a wonderful morning **market** (7 A.M.–1 P.M. daily, tourist stalls stay open later) near here on Krnarutića, where you can buy fresh produce and bread for a makeshift picnic lunch as well as a smattering of touristy souvenirs.

Narodni trg
National Square

Past the market on Krnarutića, make a right onto Jurja Barakovića towards Narodni trg, now more of a main square than the larger Forum, which once held center stage. Here you'll find a 16th-century **Gradska straža** (Guard House) with a big clock tower and the **Gradska loža** (Town Loggia, tel. 023/211-174, 9 A.M.–noon and 6–9 P.M. Mon–Fri., 9 A.M.–1 P.M. Sat., 5Kn), now an art gallery and concert venue for the town. Admission to the gallery also gets you into the **Narodni Muzej** (National Museum, Poljana Pape

Aleksandra III, tel. 023/251-851, 8 A.M.–noon and 6–9 P.M. Mon.–Fri. and 9 A.M.–1 P.M. Sat. in summer, 9 A.M.–noon and 5–8 P.M. Mon.–Fri. and 9 A.M.–1 P.M. Sat. in winter, 5Kn). The well-presented museum, located closer back toward the Port Gate (follow Široka to Poljana Pape Aleksandra III and turn right), has a display chronicling Zadar's history, paintings and relics from nearby towns, and scale models of Zadar through the centuries.

Crkva svetog Šimuna
St. Simeon's Church

Most people come to the 17th-century Crkva svetog Šimuna (Trg Šime Budinića, tel. 023/211-705, 8 A.M.–noon and 4–7 P.M. daily in summer, 8 A.M.–noon daily in winter, free) to see the opulent casket of St. Simeon. Fashioned out of some 550 pounds of silver, supported by four equally ornate bronze angels, it holds the body of St. Simeon, one of Zadar's patron saints. There are various legends surrounding the body and its casket. The body supposedly came to Zadar when a merchant shipping it from the Holy Land to Venice fell ill and died here. The identity of the body was said to be revealed to local priests in a dream. The casket, commissioned by Elizabeth, Queen of Hungary, in the late 14th century, some centuries after the death of St. Simeon in the 5th century, has a legend of its own. The story goes that she had the casket built in remorse after she stole one of the saint's fingers and it began to decompose. Once the digit was returned to its proper place, the decay miraculously stopped.

Trg pet bunara
Square of Five Wells

Trg pet bunara was once Zadar's main source of drinking water. These days it's frequented by young locals looking for a bit of recreation—summer brings frequent concerts and performances to the square. Here you'll find the **Kapetanova kula** (Captain's Tower, 10 A.M.–1 P.M. and 5–8 P.M. Mon.–Fri. and 10 A.M.–1 P.M. Sat. in summer, 10Kn), a five-sided tower built by the Venetians to defend the city against the Turks. Currently it's being used as an exhibition space for Croatian artists.

Nearby you'll find the **Kopnena vrata** (Land Gate), lined with eerie-looking cattle skulls, supposedly to scare off attackers.

Varoš Quarter

On the way back toward the Forum from Trg pet bunara, the Varoš quarter is one of Zadar's prettiest neighborhoods, filled with winding streets and little shops. The winding **Stomorica street** is packed with cafés for an afternoon coffee.

BEACHES

There's not a lot to choose from in terms of beaches in Zadar proper. Some tourists and locals swim offshore where the Sea Organ is located, but most head to **Borik,** a package-hotel mecca a short drive away (take bus #5 from Zadar, about 10 minutes). Better yet, take a ferry excursion to one of the **islands** in Zadar's archipelago.

ENTERTAINMENT AND EVENTS
Nightlife

Low-key evenings can be found in the bars and cafés around the Stomorica in the Varoš quarter, worthy of a little pub crawl. Another option is the (**Arsenal** (Trg Tri bunara 1, tel. 023/253-833, www.arsenalzadar.com, 7 A.M.–3 A.M. daily in summer, call for winter hours), which bills itself as a multipurpose arts venue. Located in a renovated 18th-century warehouse, the expansive space with soaring ceilings is the perfect place for sipping wine or a cocktail, browsing the small gallery, or listening to a local band of jazz or *klapa* singers. Arsenal also has small shops selling clothing, crafts, and local wines.

For something livelier, head to the crazy, buzz-worthy bars The Garden and Barbarella's. **The Garden** (Liburnska obala 6, tel. 023/364-739, www.thegardenzadar.com, 10 A.M.–1 A.M. daily in summer) is a British-owned club bringing in live bands and well-respected DJs to an outdoor space that's bustling both day and night. Choose from cocktails, tapas, and a solid beer list. The owners of The Garden opened **Barbarella's** (Punta Radman put 8, Petrčane, tel. 023/364-739, www.thegardenzadar.com) in 2008. The seaside location is more of an upscale young beach bar than a lounge club like The Garden.

Festivals and Events

The highlight of Zadar's summer season is the **St. Donat's Musical Evenings** (July and Aug., www.donat-festival.com) with outstanding classical concerts from international performers. Even better is the location, in the St. Donat's Church. **Zadarsko kazališno ljeto** (Zadar Theatrical Summer, late June, July, and Aug.), a mostly Croatian group of performers, and **Zadar snova** (Zadar Dreams, July and Aug.) stage theater and dance performances all over the city's historic core during the summer season.

ACCOMMODATIONS

For students and those stretching their kuna as far as possible, the **Youth Hostel Zadar** (Obala Kneza Trpimira 76, tel. 023/331-145, www.hihostels.com, beds from 78Kn), a member of Hostelling International, offers clean rooms near a beach about five kilometers north from Zadar's ancient center. If you'd like to rent a room or apartment in or around Zadar (there are even a handful in the old town), try **Marlin Tours** (Jeretova 2, tel. 023/305-920, www.marlin-tours.hr) or **Jaderatours** (Poljana Pape Aleksandra III 5/1, tel. 023/250-350, www.jaderatours.hr).

Mare Nostrum (Sveti Petar, tel. 023/391-420, www.marenostrum-hr.com, 611Kn d., including breakfast) is very simple and no frills, but a great location smack on a nice pebbly beach between Zadar and Biograd elevates it a bit.

Though you'll need to have a rental car to get the most out of a stay at the **Aparthotel Lekaviski** (Draznikova 15, tel. 023/265-888, hotel@lekavski.de, www.lekavski.de, 426Kn d.), the basic hotel has magnificent service catering to your every need. From here it's a 20-minute drive south into Zadar but just a short walk to a good beach, and the hotel can whip up excellent meals.

The outside looks like any old restaurant, but the **Hotel Niko** (Obala Kneza Domagoja 9, tel. 023/337-880, www.hotel-niko.hr, 1,306Kn d., including breakfast), located in Puntamika, a suburb north of Zadar, is a great place to stay with cozy rooms upgraded from the standard of most Croatian family hotels. It's only a few meters from the sea and it takes about 20 minutes to get into the heart of Zadar from the bus stop in front.

Though saying **Falkensteiner Club Funimation Borik** (Majstora Radovana 7, tel. 023/206-636, www.falkensteiner.com, 1,564Kn d., including three meals and use of facilities) is a bit of a mouthful, the all-inclusive hotel about 10 minutes from Zadar by car is perfect for families, with sleek rooms and family suites, a huge kids' club, playground, and mini–water park. Guests without kids can enjoy the hotel's spa services and consider booking a room in the quieter and more luxe **(Adriana wing** (1,846Kn d. all inclusive).

Built on the remains of a medieval fortress, the **(Hotel Bastion** (Bedemi zadarskih pobuna 13, tel. 023/494-950, www.hotel-bastion.hr, 1,400Kn d., including breakfast) opened in 2007. The boutique hotel is pleasant bordering on luxurious, with a waterside terrace restaurant and a small cellar-like spa. Located steps from the Sea Organ and other sights in Zadar's old town, it's convenient, pretty, and the best value in Zadar proper.

FOOD

If you're watching your kuna, try **Konoba Na Po Ure** (Špire Brusine 8, tel. 023/312-004, 9:30 A.M.–1 A.M. daily, 40Kn). Usually packed with locals and rustic ambience, the *konoba* has one of the most wallet-friendly menus (from their specialty shark to fish and grilled meats) in town. For less than 10 dollars (give or take depending on the exchange rate) you can get a full meal at **Ljepotica** (Obala kneza Branimira, tel. 023/311-288, 7 A.M.–midnight daily, no credit cards, 40Kn) near

outdoor market in Zadar

the footbridge. Choose from the daily specials (don't miss the *pašticada,* a typical Dalmatian beef dish, if it's on the menu) and enjoy a reasonably priced glass of wine. Another reliable option is **Konoba Skoblar** (Trg Petra Zoranića 4, tel. 023/213-236, 7 A.M.–midnight Mon.–Sat., 7:30 A.M.–10 P.M. Sun., 65Kn), where you can have a light snack or *marenda* of octopus salad with the regulars or go for the heartier black risotto or the *konoba*'s famous *kalelarga* cheesecake.

Had enough fish? Then head to **Pizzeria Šime** (Matije Gupca 15, tel. 023/334-848, noon–midnight daily, no credit cards, 50Kn) in Borik—nearby if you're at the Falkensteiner, not so near if you're not. The restaurant has a giant terrace and a good selection of tasty pizzas.

For more alfresco dining, **Lungo Mare** (Obala kneza Trpimira 23, tel. 023/331-533, 10:30 A.M.–midnight daily, 85Kn) has a stunning view of the sea, particularly if you're lucky enough to catch the sunset. It's a 15-minute walk north from Zadar (particularly convenient if you're staying at the Youth Hostel Zadar), but the vistas and the food and the extensive wine list make it worth the jaunt. **Kornat** (Liburnska obala 6, tel. 023/254-501, 11 A.M.–11 P.M. daily, 90Kn) is a refined place without the attitude. The wine list is excellent and the menu is peppered with gourmet features like truffles and monkfish. Don't miss the restaurant's fish stew, *na gregadu.*

On the chic and trendy side of Zadar's gastronomic offerings are two restaurants with the same owner. The first, **Dva Ribara** (Blaža Jurjeva 1, tel. 023/213-445, 10 A.M.–11 P.M. daily, 95Kn), means two fishermen, but the menu is actually stronger on the meat side of things. In the heart of town, it has a minimalist interior that contrasts nicely with the ancient surroundings. Ask for a glass of the house wine, much cheaper than the wines listed in the *vinska karta*. Dva Ribara's swankier sister, **Foša** (Kralja Dmitra Zvonimira 2, tel. 023/314-421, noon–midnight daily, 140Kn), could well belong in a much more cosmopolitan city. A staple on the restaurant scene for many years, it has had a complete overhaul that transformed the seafood restaurant into a sleek glass, wood, and chrome space with a wonderful terrace next to the city walls on a small harbor. The menu begins with a choice of 10 different kinds of olive oil, treated like wine, and goes on to include elegant versions of traditional Dalmatian cuisine, like grilled white fish with *blitva* and a few sophisticated touches like octopus carpaccio and filet mignon with truffles.

INFORMATION AND SERVICES

You can find more information, maps, advice, and free brochures from Zadar's **tourist office** (Narodni Trg, tel. 023/316-166, www.tzzadar.hr, 8 A.M.–noon daily July–Aug., 8 A.M.–8 P.M. daily June–Sept., 8 A.M.–3 P.M. Mon.–Fri. Oct.–May). Surf the Internet and have something to drink at **Arsenal** (Trg Tri bunara 1, tel. 023/253-833, www.arsenalzadar.com, 7 A.M.–3 A.M. daily). Zadar's main post office (Kralja S Držislava 1, tel. 023/316-552, 7:30 A.M.–9 P.M. Mon.–Fri., 7:30 A.M.–8 P.M. Sat.) can help you send a postcard back home.

There are three spots in town for left luggage. Try the bus station (Ante Starčevića 1, tel. 023/211-555, www.liburnija-zadar.hr, 6 A.M.–10 P.M. Mon.–Fri., 15Kn per day), the train station (Ante Starčevića 4, tel. 052/212-555, www.hznet.hr, 24 hours daily, 15Kn per day), or the Jadrolinija ferry dock (Liburnska obala 7, tel. 023/254-800, www.jadrolinija.hr, 7 A.M.–8 P.M. Mon.–Fri., 15Kn per day).

GETTING THERE AND AROUND

Zadar's airport (tel. 023/313-311, www.zadar-airport.hr) is about a 10-minute drive east from town. Croatia Airlines runs buses (25Kn) into town that coincide with their flights. If you're flying with another carrier, you can wait for the next bus or take a taxi (tel. 023/251-400, 180–220Kn).

Zadar is a large ferry port with connections to Pula (5 hours), Ancona in Italy (7 hours), and multiple points in the Zadar archipelago. Jadrolinija (Liburnska obala 7, tel. 023/254-800, www.jadrolinija.hr) runs almost all of the ferry connections.

The bus station (Ante Starčevića 1, tel. 023/211-555, www.liburnija-zadar.hr, ticket office 6 A.M.–10 P.M. daily) and train station (Ante Starčevića 4, tel. 052/212-555, www.hznet.hr, ticket office 7:30 A.M.–9 P.M. daily) are located next to each other about a 15-minute walk southeast from the old town center. You could also take local bus #5 or hop a cab (about 75Kn). Buses tend to be faster than trains for getting to Zagreb or Split. Bus connections are plentiful: Zagreb (almost two dozen daily in summer, 5 hours, 220Kn), Rijeka (6 daily in summer, 5 hours), Split (8 daily in summer, 3 hours, 120Kn) and Dubrovnik (7 daily in summer, 8 hours, 275Kn). You can also take a fast train to or from Zagreb (2 daily, 7 hours, 160Kn), though the advantage of the bus is that it's quicker and stops at Plitvice (though getting on again is slightly more difficult).

Around town, you can take the rowing boats located between the shores Liburnska obala and Obala kneza Trpirmia. Just show up and they'll shuttle you back and forth for about 7Kn. Buses to Borik are marked Puntamika. Buses to the harbor next to the old town are marked Poluotok. Bus tickets run 6Kn each way if bought from a newspaper kiosk and 10Kn if purchased onboard.

Islands Around Zadar

If you're looking for a bit of lounging seaside, some of Northern Dalmatia's most beautiful coastline is only a short ferry ride away. The islands of the Zadar archipelago are some of the least touristed in Croatia, leaving you with lots of unspoiled beauty to enjoy. Most of the islands are an easy day trip during the summer, when daily ferries connect them with Zadar's harbor. In winter it might be necessary to make an overnight trip in order to visit these wild islands.

UGLJAN

So close to Zadar it's almost a part of the city, the relatively undeveloped island of Ugljan fills up on the weekends as locals head to its shores. The island has two marinas for boaters. The **Olive Island Marina** (tel. 023/335-809, www.oliveislandmarina.com) is planning to develop a resort on the island, while the ecofriendly **Preko Marina** (tel. 023/286-169, www.marinapreko.com) is close to Preko's ferry port where buses haul travelers out to the island's villages. Hourly ferries from Zadar take about 30 minutes and cost around 20Kn.

Beaches near the ferry dock get very crowded. Ask the **tourist office** (tel. 023/286-8388, tzpreko@preko.hr, www.preko.hr) in Preko about renting a bike to explore the less-developed western side of the island, or find a water taxi to take you out to the islet of **Galevac**, just offshore, for some of the best swimming. Galevac has a 15th-century monastery and nice beaches backed by thick woods to provide a bit of shade.

Your best option for accommodation on Ugljan is a private room or apartment, booked by visiting the local tourist office on Preko's main square or via their website. The **Konoba Barbara** (Put Jerolimovih 4, tel. 023/286-129, noon–midnight daily, closed Nov.–Mar., 60Kn) is one good option for grilled fish dishes and salads.

PAŠMAN

The sleepy little island of Pašman has some friendly fishing villages and a 12th-century fortress that's now a monastery, in the village of Ugrinći. For swimming, try the coast south of **Tkon,** the busiest town on the island. There you'll discover plenty of sandy shores near the Sovinje nudist resort. If you'd rather your fellow bathers stay clothed, the pebbled beaches of Lučina, on the northern side of the island near Pašman Village, are another option.

If you're inclined to stay overnight try the campsite on the island, **Lučina** (tel. 023/260-173, www.lucina.hr, 80Kn), or book a private room through the **tourist office** (tel. 023/260-155, www.pasman.hr). There are a couple of friendly, clean pensions in town, such as the **Apartmani Lanterna** (Pašman Village, Obala bb, tel. 023/260-179, www.lanterna.hr, 390Kn d.) or the **Vila Kruna** (Kraj 122a, tel. 023/285-410, www.vila-kruna.com, 425Kn d.). The Lanterna also has a good restaurant with fresh fish, most of which is cooked in a stone oven.

You'll get to Pašman by taking the ferry from Zadar to Ugljan and then hopping a bus (almost 10 daily in summer, 25 minutes). The bus first stops in Pašman Village and ends at Tkon, the island's official center.

IŽ

Iž is a tiny, slightly unkempt-in-a-good-way island with two main villages, Veli Iž and Mali Iž. There's not much to do here besides swim, eat, and hike the paths cutting through the slightly wild olive trees. Also near Zadar and serviced by a daily car ferry (which lets off in Bršanj, not the best village if you don't have a car) or the weekly ferries (which let out in the much more developed Veli Iž), the island is relatively undeveloped, leaving private rooms and apartments the best options for accommodation. Try the **Apartmani Švorinić Venka** (tel. 023/278-160, www.svorinic-venka.com, 355Kn d.), which has clean basic rooms, some with sea views, in Mali Iž, or the **Apartmani Strgačić** (tel. 023/319-484, www.apartmani-strgacic.hr, 285Kn d.) in Veli Iž, which also organizes fishing expeditions.

The **Hotel Korinjak** (tel. 023/277-064, www.korinjak.hr, 3,906Kn d. per week, including all meals) is a typical relic of the Tito days, a big concrete block in a good location with basic rooms and basic service. Rooms are only rented on a weekly basis.

There's a smattering of restaurants down by the harbor where you can get a good meal or a strong coffee.

◖ DUGI OTOK

With a name that literally means long island and at 50 kilometers in length and 4.5 kilometers in width, Dugi Otok is the largest of the islands forming the Zadar archipelago. Dugi Otok is arguably its prettiest as well, with a quirky geography forming dozens of indented coves and cliff-backed coastline. The biggest draw for the island is the **Telašćica Bay** nature park (Ulica Danijela Grbin bb, Sali, tel. 023/377-096, www.telascica.hr, 30Kn), where you'll find some nice swimming and a saltwater lake, **Jezero mira.** The park is just a few kilometers out of the village of Sali, a great distance for a bike ride if you don't have a car (and perhaps even if you do).

If you're looking for something a little less quiet, try the sandy **Sahuran beach** just south of Veli Rat.

The best accommodation on the island is in private rooms and apartments, which can be booked through the island's **tourist office** (Obala Perta Lorinija bb, tel. 023/377-094, tz-sali@zd.t-com.hr, www.dugiotok.hr, 8 A.M.–9 P.M. daily July–Aug., 8 A.M.–3 P.M. Mon.–Fri. Sept.–May) located in the village of Sali. The **Hotel Maxim** (tel. 023/291-291, www.hoteli-bozava.hr, 1,165Kn d., including breakfast and dinner) is another option for an overnight. Reconstructed and decked out with a slightly garish facade, the hotel has a nice swimming pool and is located directly on the sea. For a nice tavern atmosphere and good local fish specialties, try **Kod Sipe** (Sali 174, tel. 023/377-137, 10 A.M.–midnight in summer, call for winter hours, 80Kn) or ◖ **Tavern Go-Ro** (Uvala Telašćica, tel. 098/853-434, 10 A.M.–midnight, closed Oct.–Apr., 70Kn) in Telašćica Bay, with a beautiful view and fish stew and lamb *ispod peka* (call three hours in advance to order lamb).

Taking a day trip to Dugi Otok is really only a possibility in summer (June–Aug.), since ferry connections from Zadar (1.5 hours) get rather sporadic the rest of the year. There are at least two ferries daily in summer (check with the Jadrolinija office in Zadar's harbor) letting off at points like Brbinj, Božava, and Sali. Buses between the towns are few and infrequent, so if you're traveling without a car, try to get a ferry that docks in Sali, the best entry point to the Telašćica Bay park, or Zaglav, where a bus to Sali meets the ferry.

SILBA

This car-free island, the northernmost island of the Zadar archipelago, is filled with lots of peaceful coves and beaches, perfect for bikers and families. The peaceful part is somewhat altered in summer when the year-round population of several hundred is augmented by lots of tourists and locals that descend on the elegant little Silba, lined with patrician merchants' houses and courtyard gardens from its seafaring days. Beaches to the west of Silba Town are definitely the prettiest and offer some spectacular sunsets. The island's **tourist office** (tel. 023/370-010, www.silba.net, 8 A.M.–noon Mon.–Sat. July–Aug., call for off-season hours) has a list of private rooms and apartments. For nourishment try **Konoba Mul** (Port mul, tel. 023/370-351, 11 A.M.–11 P.M. daily July–Aug., call for hours at other times, 75Kn), serving good fish dishes and salads in pleasant surroundings next to the bobbing boats in the little harbor.

There are several boat connections daily with Silba in the summer months. Zadar has the most, though note that the catamarans (1.75 hours) are the fastest. The car ferries can take around 3.5 hours since they have other stops to make. It's also possible to connect with Pula (6 connections weekly in summer), Rijeka (1 connection weekly in summer), and Lošinj (6 connections weekly in summer). Contact Jadrolinija (www.jadrolinija.hr) about current schedules and prices.

Paklenica National Park

Paklenica National Park, founded in 1949, is the best place for trekking through the craggy karst landscape of Northern Dalmatia. Just a couple of kilometers from beaches and package-holiday hotels, nature lovers can lose themselves (hopefully not literally, though) in the park's gorges, peaks, and caves. The park also offers wonderful opportunities for rock-climbing fans and the less-active traveler can still take advantage of the rocky wilderness on an off-road safari.

The small town of **Starigrad Paklenica** is the best base for seeing the park and as a center for accommodation and food. Buses connecting Rijeka and Zadar usually stop in Starigrad Paklenica (note that many locals will refer to it simply as Starigrad, but it's best to add the Paklenica to keep it from getting mistaken for another Starigrad near Senj). The park is about two kilometers north of the town.

At the entrance to the park, you can buy tickets at the ticket booth (40Kn in high season for a one-day entrance, additional 15Kn for entrance to the Manita Peć cave) and pick up a free map of the park's trails, or visit the **park office** (Dr. F. Tudmana 14a, tel. 023/369-202, www.paklenica.hr, call for hours particularly in autumn–spring) in Starigrad Paklenica before setting out. The office sells detailed maps and can help you plan your trip.

SPORTS AND RECREATION
Hiking and Tours

Paklenica is filled with some 150 kilometers of mapped hiking routes. Most routes will take at least two hours round-trip, though you can wind your way through the park for a few days if you like. Just after you leave the ticket booth, you'll see the **Paklenički mlinovi** (Paklenica Mills, 8 A.M.–7 P.M. daily in summer, by arrangement with the park office out of season). The seven corn- and grain-grinding mills were in use up until the 1960s, serving the area and even the outlying islands. Today there are demonstrations of the water-driven mills, as long as the water flow is heavy enough to operate them.

Continuing up the main trail, following the Velika Paklenica gorge, you'll find a series of underground **tunnels** built by the Yugoslav government to shelter high-level officials in the event of an emergency. At the time of this writing, the tunnels are closed due to construction, but the park plans to open them in the future for events and exhibitions.

Serious hikers will not be put off by the challenging climb to reach the **Manita Peć cave**. The cave must be visited with a park **guide** (guided tours 10 A.M.–1 P.M. Sat. in April, 10 A.M.–1 P.M. Wed. and Sat. in May, 10 A.M.–1 P.M. Mon., Wed., and Sat. in June and Oct., 10 A.M.–1 P.M. daily July–Sept., by arrangement other months of the year, 15Kn). The trip will take about 1.5 hours one-way to see the 175-meter-long cave filled with lots of dripping stalactites and stalagmites.

The mountain has a small rest stop for

BURA WINDS

You'll hear it talked about all over Croatia's Adriatic coast. The *bura* is a cold – sometimes bitterly so – northerly or northeasterly wind that can chill you even on a sunny winter's day on the islands. That's not to say the *bura* can't blow any time of year, but it's that extra cold, gusting wind in winter that really seems to get talked about. The Velebit mountain range is the hardest hit by the *bura*; Kvarner is second in line. The *bura* can come out of nowhere. One moment it's calm and clear and a few hours later winds (in the range of 200 kilometers per hour) are whipping against sailboats and bridges, making all forms of transportation hazardous.

However, the *bura* actually contributes to a lot of the character of the coastal regions. Most of the towns are built densely with narrow streets to counteract the winds. And it's the winds that cure the area's top-quality *pršut* as well.

climbing on limestone rock in Paklenica National Park

snacks and drinks, the **Forest Hut Lugarnica** (10:30 A.M.–4:30 P.M. daily June–Sept., 10:30 A.M.–4:30 P.M. weekends Apr.–May and Oct.), about a two-hour walk from the parking lot depending on which path you take.

For those who don't want to go it alone, the park offers half-day and full-day guided tours as well as specialized tours for bird-watchers. The tours can be arranged in advance through the park office.

There are several options for those who don't want to trek for hours at a time but want to see the beauty of the Velebit Mountains. The tourist office in Starigrad Paklenica can hook you up with agencies providing **boat trips** up the Zrmanja River and the owner of the Hotel Rajna organizes **photo safaris** (tel. 023/369-130, www.hotel-rajna.com) through the Velebit in four-wheel-drive vehicles.

Climbing

Paklenica National Park is a great spot for rock climbers, with some 400 routes, both single-pitch and multi-pitch, available. The park also hosts an international competition, **Mammut Big Wall Speed Climbing,** every late April/early May. The park office also sells a detailed climbing guide. It's often best to forget about climbing in the winter months when strong *bura* winds might just blow you off the cliff.

ACCOMMODATIONS

Most accommodation will be found in the village of Starigrad Paklenica, though the park has its own **Camp National Park** (Dr. F. Tuđmana 14a, tel. 023/369-202, www.paklenica.hr, from 40Kn per person), located on a stretch of pebbly beach next to the main park office in Starigrad Paklenica. Due to the small size of the camp, reservations are not possible. The Paklenica National Park does not allow camping within its borders, but for those hoping for a longer trek it does offer the **Paklenica Mountain Hut** (tel. 023/213-792 or check at the park office for reservations, 70Kn per person) with a common sleeping room, a kitchen, and a dining hall. You will need to bring your own sleeping bag and supplies.

For slightly cushier digs, the friendly family

Hotel Rajna (Ul. Dr. F. Tuđmana 105, tel. 023/369-130, www.hotel-rajna.com, 340Kn d., including breakfast) is quite a comfy two-star hotel with most basic creature comforts. If you're traveling with friends or want to splurge a bit, the owner also has a charming ◖ **stone cottage Varoš** (tel. 023/369-130, www.hotel-rajna.com, cottage rental 1,986Kn per night, sleeps 15) a 15-minute walk to Paklenica National Park. The 1850-era building is furnished tastefully and traditionally.

FOOD

The restaurant at the **Hotel Rajna** (Jadranska cesta 105, tel. 023/359-121, 6:30 A.M.–11 P.M. daily, closed first two weeks in Jan., 85Kn) has good grilled fish and meats and fish stew. However, the real treat in Starigrad Paklenica is ◖ **4 Ferala** (Joze Dokoze 20, tel. 023/369-304, www.hotel-vicko.hr, 7 A.M.–11 P.M. daily, 95Kn) in the Vičko Hotel, specializing in Dalmatian traditional dishes from roast lamb to mussels in a garlic and wine sauce.

GETTING THERE AND AROUND

Paklenica National Park is located about 200 kilometers south of Rijeka and 45 kilometers north of Zadar on the coastal road. If you're driving, head to Starigrad Paklenica and then follow the signs to the entrance of Paklenica Park (brown signs labeled N.P. Paklenica), about two kilometers north of Starigrad Paklenica. Parking is available at the entrance to the park; there's another lot past the info point, which is the better option.

Buses between Rijeka and Zadar will often stop at Starigrad Paklenica to pick up passengers (unless they're full, which can happen often in the summer); they'll drop you off if you ask. From Zagreb, the best bet is to take a bus to Zadar and connect with Starigrad Paklenica (1.25 hours, 28Kn). There is no public transportation to Paklenica National Park; those without a car will have to walk the two kilometers from Starigrad Paklenica to the park.

Plitvice Lakes National Park

One of Croatia's biggest tourist attractions, the 16 lakes comprising Plitvice Lakes National Park are some of Croatia's most stunning scenery. Though the park is technically inland, travelers most often stop off on their way to or from the coast or via excursions offered from coastal towns.

Plitvice has long been a tourist destination; in the late 19th century visitors started to arrive to admire the natural wonders. The park was under Serb control from 1991 to 1995, with forces using the hotels as barracks. It didn't take long to repair the damage to the buildings and flood the area with travelers once again.

The color of the lakes can be turquoise blue or deep green and the park is filled with giant trees and lots of wildlife. Formed by thousands of years of calcium carbonate deposits, the lakes are held by a natural travertine dam that grows at least a little each year. The lakes were declared a national park by Yugoslavia in 1949. A UNESCO World Heritage site since 1979, with close to one million tourists seeing the lakes every year, the park is definitely worth a visit. It's also easy to visit, with dozens of paths, lots of information, and an organized system of shuttle buses and boats that's included in the entrance fee.

SIGHTS

Plitvice Lakes National Park (tel. 053/751-015, www.np-plitvice-jezera.hr, 8 A.M.–7 P.M. daily May–Sept., dawn–dusk Oct.–Apr., 110Kn Apr.–Oct., 70Kn Nov.–Mar.) has two entrances from the old Zagreb–Split road. Both entrances have helpful information centers, though Entrance 2 (closest to area accommodation) is often closed in winter. As you walk along the paths and bridges keep an eye out for wildlife, particularly birds (there are over 100 varieties).

Donja jezera
Lower Lakes

Entrance 1 (Ulaz jedan) on the northern end of the park is considered the main entry point. It's here that you're closest to the most-touristed spot, tall Veliki Slap (Big Waterfall). It's about a 10-minute walk to Veliki Slap; paths from there can take you to other waterfalls or to the shuttle boat toward Entrance 2.

The lower lakes include Kaluđerovac Lake, Gavanovac Lake, and Milanovac Lake, small lakes punctuated by waterfalls and a couple of caves (near Kaluđerovac Lake). These feed into the large Kozjak Lake, the largest of Plitvice's bodies of water and the border between the lower and upper lakes.

At the top of Kozjak you'll have the option of taking a shuttle (included in your entrance fee) to Entrance 2, at the southern end of Kozjak, or to continue along the footpath on the eastern shore.

Gornja jezera
Upper Lakes

Reached by trekking about five kilometers from Entrance 1 or by Entrance 2 (Ulaz dva) to its south, the upper lakes are some of Plitvice's most beautiful and also not quite as busy. Near the park's hotels you'll find Gradinsko Lake and then Galovac Lake, where the water descends like stairs, dropping into a series of sparkling blue pools. Galovac is followed by Okrugljak Lake, where waterfalls take center stage, and then Ciginovac Lake and Prošćansko Lake. If all the uphill walking is just too much, a good idea is to take the shuttle from Entrance 2 to Okrugljak Lake and then walk down.

ACCOMMODATIONS AND FOOD

A good choice for budget travelers, **Camp Korana** (tel. 053/751-888, www.np-plitvicka-jezera.hr, 227Kn d. for bungalow, including breakfast) has spots for tents as well as small private bungalows (actually huts), with communal bathrooms. The main downside to the camp is that it's about six kilometers from the park entrance. Try to grab a spot at the simple **Villa Mukinja** (Mukinje 47, tel. 01/652-1857, www.plitvice-lakes.com, 425Kn d., including breakfast and dinner); it's the place to stay in Plitvice. It's a 10-minute walk to the park, and the price includes a good breakfast and dinner, basic but clean rooms, and wireless Internet access. The small hotel doesn't have air-conditioning, which is normally not a problem since the area cools down considerably at night, but that might be a consideration during a heat wave. The **Plitvice Hotel** (tel. 053/751-100, www.np-plitvicka-jezera.hr, 700Kn d., including breakfast) has an excellent location, just a five-minute walk to the park; its communist-era time warp can be an experience in itself. Don't stay for the rooms or the sub-par food (run elsewhere for dinner) but for the convenience.

There are several restaurants around Entrance 2, though the best is across from Entrance 1, the **Lička kuća** (Entrance 1, tel. 053/751-024, 11 A.M.–11 P.M. daily Apr.–Oct., 85Kn), with lots of regional specialties and traditional hearty food like spicy sausage stew. The place is touristy but it's also very good. Even better is to buy some bread and fresh tomatoes from the supermarket and local **homemade cheese** from the usually present vendors. The rounds are typically sold whole but if you ask for half *(pola)* you'll probably strike a deal. The cheese has a slightly nutty, smoky flavor that hits just the right chord on a crisp night.

GETTING THERE AND AROUND

Plitvice is located about 90 kilometers south of Karlovac and 160 kilometers northeast of Zadar. If you're driving to Plitvice, just follow the signs from the highway or the old coastal road. Arriving by bus is fairly easy—most buses going from Zagreb (2.5 hours) to Split (3.5 hours) or other Dalmatian cities will stop here as they pass by; they'll drop you off if you ask, stopping in front of either of the two entrances. Getting back on a bus can be trickier since there's not much in the way of schedules and they won't stop if they're full. As a result, if you don't have a car, it's probably best to book a Plitvice excursion trip (around 350Kn), advertised widely at travel agencies all along the coast.

Murter and the Kornati Islands

If you've ever wondered what it would be like to live on a deserted island, you can probably find a spot in the Kornati archipelago, a largely wild national park, to answer any lingering questions. The town of Murter is the gateway to the islands and also a spot for accommodation before embarking on your journey.

MURTER

There's nothing much to say about Murter except that it's the handiest point of departure for the Kornati archipelago. Since Kornati doesn't have a lot in the way of accommodation, you're more likely to have luck here, planning your trip from the **Kornati National Park office** (Butina 2, tel. 022/435-740, www.kornati.hr, 8 A.M.–3 P.M. Mon.–Fri. June–Sept., call for hours in winter), which sells permits for diving and fishing as well as maps, or from local agencies where you can rent a boat or book an excursion. The agency **KornatTurist** (Hrvatskih vladara 2, tel. 022/435-854, www.kornatturist.hr) can also help you arrange private rooms and accommodation on the island. **Eseker Tours** (Majnova bb, tel. 022/435-669, www.esekertours.hr) rents all sorts of things like bikes (60Kn a day), scooters (45Kn an hour), boats (from 300Kn/day for a simple fishing boat to 2,900Kn/day for an extra-fancy motorboat), and personal watercraft (75Kn for 10 minutes).

For dining try **Tic-Tac** (Vlade Hrokešina 5, tel. 022/435-230, noon–11 P.M. daily, closed Oct.–Apr., reservations recommended, 85Kn), on a small street not far from the main square. The decor is simple but the menu is nothing less than gourmet. Dishes like tuna carpaccio, cuttlefish in black sauce with polenta, and gnocchi with fish roe and prawns are surprisingly sophisticated for such an unassuming little place.

Getting to Murter is easiest from Šibenik or Vodice. Buses (7–10 a day) connect to the island, conveniently disembarking at Murter's main square. There are also several ferries connecting from Šibenik and Zadar (check with Jadrolinija, www.jadrolinija.hr, for times and prices).

KORNATI ISLANDS

The Kornati Islands stretch out south of Zadar's coast. The archipelago was declared a national park in 1980 and remains one of the most stunning land- and seascapes in Croatia. Though the islands were once covered with oak trees, those were burned to make way for sheep pastures. Instead of taking away the beauty of the islands, it might have made them prettier. The bright-white slightly scruffy karst rock formations are a beautiful contrast with the clear blue waters, which are home to lots of local fish such as bream, eel, sea scorpion, and cuttlefish. The waters around the islands, particularly the eastern edges if the sea is not too rough, are a wonderful place to snorkel or scuba dive.

There's proof of Illyrian and Roman settlements on the islands, though the islands were mostly uninhabited, owned by Zadar's aristocracy until the 19th century. After that, locals from the islands of Murter used them to raise sheep. Sheep aren't tended on the islands today, but you'll see some wild ancestors (though significantly less since some 1,300 died during the drought of 2007), as well as a number of abandoned stone cottages (mostly dating from the early to mid-20th century), occasionally inhabited in summer by their owners from Murter, who defected long ago. Other than the sheep, there's not a lot of wildlife save for the occasion lizard, snake, or bird.

The islands are immensely popular with yachters, so though there's not a lot of accommodation, there are multiple places to choose from for an amazing seafood lunch or dinner. If you'd like to stay on Kornati, you can rent one of the abandoned stone cottages through an agency in Murter, who will leave you there for several days with a stash of supplies, in case you ever wanted to see for yourself what it's like on one of those reality shows.

Food

Whether it's thanks to the number of yachts and fancy sailboats that cruise around Kornati, occasionally mooring in the coves and harbors, or simply a local sensibility for good food—or some of each—the fact remains that Kornati is a treasure trove of excellent restaurants. There are at least 17 restaurants in the uninhabited island chain, almost one for every nautical mile. Not fancy restaurants, mind you—you're likely to sit on plastic chairs. But you'll have an awesome view and cuisine that would satisfy even the toughest food critic. Best of all, you can tie your boat up right in front, eat to your heart's content, and then keep on sailing. One note: The restaurants don't really have menus (they basically fix whatever they've caught). Figure on paying somewhere between 80Kn and 120Kn for a main dish, much more for lobster.

Katina Island: Mare's (Vela Proversa, tel. 098/273-873, www.restaurant-mare.com, 10 A.M.–midnight daily, no credit cards) has been a fixture on Kornati since the 1950s; the family who owns it has been on the island since the 19th century. The family still tends a grove of olive trees, producing sweet organic oil, and they grow the vegetables served alongside the main dishes. If it's available, try the *Brudet od ljutice i janjetina s krumpirom* (shallot soup and lamb with potatoes).

Strižnja Bay, Kornat Island: The menu at **Darko's** (Uvala Strižnja, no phone, 8 A.M.–midnight daily, closed Oct.–Mar., no credit cards) is quite simple—you'll get whatever it is that Darko caught that day, baked or broiled, alongside fish soup and octopus salad. In fact, the owner makes it a principle to never serve less than the best quality, so if you want lamb here, you'd better come in the spring when it's at its most tender.

Vrulje, Kornat Island: Ante's (Uvala Vrulje, tel. 022/435-025, 10 A.M.–midnight daily, no credit cards) is a back-to-basics restaurant run by a true fisherman. The octopus *(hobotnica)* à la Veneziana, a thick tomato-based stew with more than a hint of red wine, is highly recommended.

Opat Cove, Kornat Island: A stone house with green shutters nestled on a rocky, barren hill is the location for **Opat** (Uvala Opat, Luke 47, tel. 022/435-061, 9 A.M.–midnight daily), a family restaurant known for its brick oven-baked seafood, like scorpionfish with potatoes. Some of the dishes seem highly creative, like fish soaked in milk before cooking then seasoned with mustard and fennel, or the sea-egg risotto, though the atmosphere is totally laid-back.

Vela Smokvica Island: Located in a deep blue cove, **Piccolo** (Obala Smokvica Vela, tel. 022/435-106, 7 A.M.–midnight daily, closed Oct.–Apr., no credit cards) is one of the islands' most popular restaurants. It's a family-run business: The wife cooks what the husband catches. Dine on lots of fresh grilled seafood, or fish stew seasoned with paprika.

Getting There and Around

There are no ferries to Kornati. If you'd like to visit you have two choices: Travel on your own boat (you'll need an international captain's license) or take an organized tour of the islands. Tours can be booked through the many agencies in Murter, such as **KornatTurist** (Hrvatskih vladara 2, tel. 022/435-854, www.kornatturist.hr), or by signing up with one of the clipboard-wielding young people along Murter's harbor. Most of the excursions include a tour, a swim, and lunch for around 250Kn per person. If you'd like to explore the island with more freedom and you don't have a captain's license, inquire in Murter at the **Kornati National Park office** (Butina 2, tel. 022/435-740, www.kornati.hr, 8 A.M.–3 P.M. Mon.–Fri. June–Sept., call for hours in winter).

Šibenik

One of the most overlooked towns in the country, Šibenik has a wonderful old town, not too packed with tourists even at the height of the season and with some great finds in accommodation. An important location in Venice's fight to hold off the Turks, the town flourished in the Middle Ages, and in modern times as well, when a big aluminum plant kept the locals employed. However, the war in the 1990s changed all of that, with the plant drying up (now a decaying relic along the Magistrala) and the city falling on hard times.

Most Croatians would probably wrinkle their noses if you mention Šibenik, since it's never really been thought of as a tourist destination. There are no resorts to speak of, no real beaches. So why would you go?

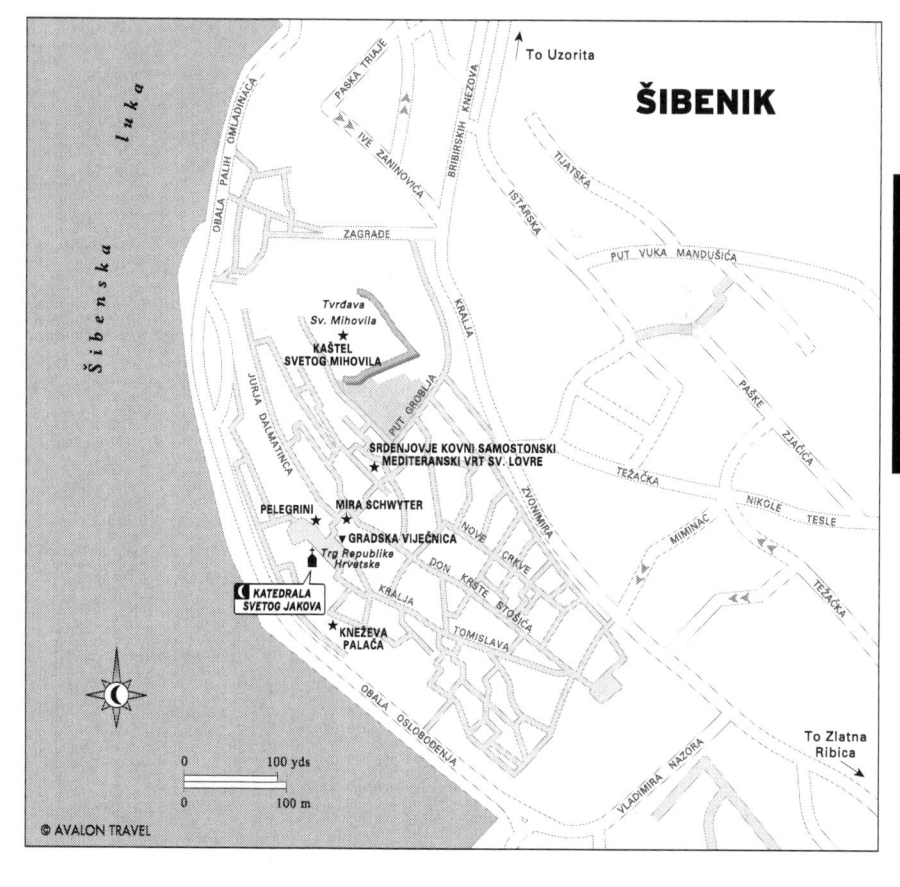

The old town center, for one, is totally charming and almost perfectly preserved, yet it doesn't have any of the made-for-tourists feel that many other cities with lots of original buildings have. Though you won't find any mega-resorts, the center is packed with character-filled apartments where you can live like a local during your vacation, heading down to one of the town's best cafés for breakfast and a coffee with the other regulars. And who needs a town beach when you can walk down to the ferry dock and hop a boat for a 20-minute or one-hour ride to an island almost devoid of cars, with wild, natural beaches, way less crowded than any near the resorts.

Basically, if you know how to work Šibenik you'll love it, particularly if you're a contrarian who likes to stay away from tourist-laden spots.

SIGHTS
◉ Katedrala svetog Jakova
St. Jacob's Cathedral

Outshining all of the town's pretty architecture and churches, the 15th-century Katedrala svetog Jakova (Trg Republike Hrvatske, tel. 022/214-899, 9:30 A.M.–8 P.M. Mon.–Sat. and 1–8 P.M. Sun. July–Aug., 9 A.M.–6:30 P.M. Mon.–Sat. and 1–6 P.M. Sun. Sept.–May, free) glows over Šibenik's old-town waterfront. The church was built by local architect Juraj

Katedrala svetog Jakova

JURAJ DALMATINAC, FAMED ARCHITECT

Dalmatia's most famous stone mason and architect, Juraj Dalmatinac, put his stamp on churches and buildings up and down Croatia's coast. He was born in Dalmatia around the year 1400, and studied his trade in Venice, where he had an atelier and contributed to carvings on the Doge's Palace. In Italy he was known as Giorgio da Sebenico (or George of Šibenik); he returned to Dalmatia with his first big commission for the Šibenik cathedral. He settled down here, building a house in town, but due to lack of funding the cathedral project often stalled, and he spent the time working on other projects up and down the coast. His touch is found on several palaces in Split as well as an altar in the Split cathedral, the Minčeta Fortress in Dubrovnik, and a loggia in Ancona, Italy, among others. He died in 1473, the Šibenik cathedral still unfinished. A statue of Dalmatinac by Meštrović stands across from the cathedral, looking over the water.

Dalmatinac, among others, since it took over 100 years to complete. The inside is luxurious, with lots of gilt and a soaring ceiling topped by an octagonal dome. The most interesting features, however, are on the Gothic and Renaissance facade. The building is encircled by 71 stone heads—according to legend the faces of those townspeople who didn't pony up for the construction, making the addition of the dog head all the more humorous. The top of the dome itself is beautiful, with a gilt-topped cupola and four somber statues guarding the town and sea below, but it's hard to catch a glimpse of them unless you climb the steps next to the loggia (above Trg Republike Hrvatske) and look back from the top.

Kneževa palača
Duke's Palace

To the south of St. Jacob's Cathedral down a

small alleyway, you'll come to the 15th-century Kneževa palača. Inside, the **Muzej grada Šibenika** (City Museum, Gradska vrata 3, tel. 022/213-880, www.muzej-sibenik.hr) has exhibits on a variety of historical periods and persons such as architect Juraj Dalmatinac. The museum's permanent collection, however, was in storage at the time of writing, while the space undergoes renovations. It's due to reopen in 2009.

Trg Republike Hrvatske
Republic of Croatia Square

The large square to the eastern side of St. Jacob's Cathedral is the Trg Republike Hrvatske, flanked by the town hall and its 16th-century **loggia**, today home to a café. To the north of the cathedral you'll find the delightful **Bunari Museum** (Palih omladinica 2, tel. 022/485-055, 8 A.M.–midnight daily May–Sept., 15Kn), located in a 15th-century water-storage facility. Today visitors can walk through a display of Šibenik's past; younger guests will get the most out of the multimedia exhibit. There's also a small café with revolving art exhibits.

Srdenjovje kovni samostanski mediteranski vrt Sv. Lovre
Medieval Mediterranean Garden of St. Lawrence's Monastery

Opened in 2007, the Srdenjovje kovni samostanski mediteranski vrt Sv. Lovre (Strme stube 1, tel. 022/212-515, www.spg.hr, 8 A.M.–11 P.M. in summer, call for winter hours, 15Kn) re-creates a medieval garden, heavy on herbs and indigenous plants. A must for gardeners, it's also the perfect place to have a coffee or a drink among the fragrant lavender and thyme on your way to or from the city's old fortress.

Kaštel svetog Mihovila
St. Michael's Fortress

From pretty much anywhere in the old town you can climb up to the northeast to find Kaštel svetog Mihovila (approx. 9 A.M.–dusk, 10Kn), a crumbling Venetian fortress most noteworthy for its peaceful views out over the bay. Considering the medieval town plan, one of the most straightforward ways to get there is to follow the Strme Stube to the Medieval Mediterranean Garden and keep climbing, following the signs marked Kaštel.

Etnoland

Though it bills itself as Croatia's first theme park, Etnoland (Postolarsko 6, Drniš, tel. 099/220-0205, www.dalmati.com, daily mid-Mar.–mid-Nov., call to reserve a tour, from 30Kn without lunch) is actually more of a historical village. In Drniš, a short drive from Šibenik, visitors leave behind modern times in the parking lot as they embark on a journey through traditional Dalmatian life, learning about celebrations, customs, and crafts, and seeing mock-ups of houses from a century ago. Though you can wander through the park alone, most guests book a tour that lasts 3.5 hours and includes a traditional Dalmatian

---

TWO DAYS IN ŠIBENIK

DAY 1
Arriving in the afternoon, visit the **cathedral** and perhaps a museum before making a beeline for the **Medieval Mediterranean Garden of St. Lawrence's Monastery** for a coffee among the fragrant herbs. Head to **Pelegrini** for dinner, preferably in the courtyard, making sure to order a starter of cheese, *pršut*, and local olives along with a glass of wine.

DAY 2
After a night in your old-town apartment, start the morning at Pelegrini again, this time snagging a table around 9 A.M. on the stairs overlooking the cathedral and the water. Linger with coffee until your ferry leaves for **Zlarin** or **Prvić**. Spend the day soaking up the sun and salt-tinged breeze before returning to Šibenik in the evening. Have dinner on the vine-surrounded terrace of **Uzorita** to top off a perfect day.

lunch. The park opened in 2007, and is well thought out if a bit touristy. The Jurlinovi dvori on the hills of nearby Primošten are more authentic in feel.

BEACHES

Šibenik itself has nothing in the way of beaches, but there are plenty of nearby spots for sun and surf, making the city an easy point of departure. A few beaches are accessible by car, though unless you're with the kids there's little to recommend them. The Solaris hotel complex (drive south of town on the Magistrala and look for the signs or take bus #6) has a sandy beach, a new bar area constructed of authentic stone huts, and plenty of video games and bouncy castles for the little ones. However, the best beaches are a short water taxi or ferry ride away. First up and closest to Šibenik's center is the tiny island of **Zlarin,** known for its coral jewelry; it's about 20 minutes across the water to reach Zlarin. There's an excellent *konoba* at the end of the marina's dock and two shops specializing in expensive (or overpriced, given your view) coral jewelry; they fill to capacity as soon as every ferry lands. Otherwise the island is super quiet, with a small pebbly beach to the left of the marina if you're facing the island and concrete bathing areas further on. Keep walking around to find a really wild and beautiful stretch of deserted beach, not so good for swimming given the winds and the rocks, but perfect for wading and lounging in solitude.

Another choice of island excursions is the slightly farther afield **Prvić** (45-minute ferry journey from Šibenik), a car-free island covered with pines and herbs sprouting out of rocky stretches. The best beach on the island is at **Šepurine.** If you'd like to stay overnight unlike the hordes of day-tripping tourists, the simple but lovely **Hotel Maestral** (tel. 022/448-300, www.hotelmaestral.com, 298Kn d., including breakfast), located in an old stone house in Prvić Luka, is a great spot.

Šibenik's harbor is the spot to catch the (usually) twice-daily ferries to the islands. Check with the Jadrolinija office at the harbor for schedules and prices, since even the schedule posted outside the office is not always correct.

ENTERTAINMENT AND EVENTS
Nightlife

Though Šibenik's not known for its partying scene, the club **Inside** (Bioci, no phone,

the island of Zlarin, known for its coral jewelry

7 A.M.–midnight Mon.–Wed., 7 A.M.–4 A.M. Fri.–Sat., 7 A.M.–1 A.M. Sun.) has lots of space for dancing and clubbing in a converted military building on the road to Split. The view's not much to speak of but the crowd is more local than what you'll find at most bars up and down the coast. Back in town try the bars on the seafront in the old town for a post-dinner drink.

Festivals and Events

If you're looking for a bit of Dalmatian flavor in Šibenik, Thursday evenings in July and August bring out local *klapa* **groups** (contact the tourist office at Obala Dr. Franje Tuđmana 5, tel. 022/214-411, www.sibenik-tourism.hr, for more details). The end of August is heralded by two days of varied musical performances during the **Večeri Dalmatinske Šansone** (Dalmatian Chanson Evenings, www.sansona-sibenik.com), though the city's biggest event is the **Međunarodni Dječji Festival** (International Children's Festival, www.mdf-si.org), held for two weeks from the end of June to the beginning of July every year since 1958. The town hosts dozens of performances, art exhibitions, and hands-on educational exhibits, all revolving around children.

Shoppers will appreciate the weekly **antiques fair** (around the Crkve Svetog Frane, http://sibenik.antikviteti.net, 8 A.M.–3 P.M. Sat.), which operates additional days in the summer.

ACCOMMODATIONS

Šibenik is surrounded by several hotels and apartments that are, for the most part, overpriced and under-performing. If you're on a tight budget, check with the **Cromovens agency** (Trg Republike Hrvatske 4, tel. 022/212-515, www.cromovens.hr), on the Trg Republike Hrvatske near St. Jacob's Cathedral, about private rooms and apartments. Just be sure to check their distance from public transportation, as most are not located within walking distance of the old town (or anything else, for that matter).

The best options are apartments in Šibenik's ancient core. **C Ms. Mira Schwyter** (tel. 091/211-0962, mira.schwyter@si.t-com.hr, www.bedandbreakfastdalmatia.com, 690Kn d., including breakfast at Pelegrini) rents out two beautiful apartments, located in a historic 15th-century building that had a previous life as a café and art gallery. Paintings still hang on the wall available for purchase as pricey souvenirs, alongside photos of famous actors and local musicians, all guests of the former café. Each apartment has antique furniture, stone walls, air-conditioning, and a small kitchen and bath. Second on the list of apartments are the **Konoba** (Andrije Kacića 8, tel. 091/198-8989, www.bbdalmatia.com, 533Kn d.) owned by a lovely Dutch family and decorated simply but tastefully. One of the apartments has a wonderful balcony with a view over the old town's roof tops, though it does lack air-conditioning.

FOOD

In the heart of the old town try **Konoba Dalmatino** (Fra Nikole Ružića 1, tel. 091/542-4808, generally open 11 A.M.–10 P.M. daily in summer, call for winter hours, 75Kn), nestled in a narrow alleyway with a handful of outdoor tables serving good cheese, salads, and fish dishes alongside the potable house wine—not the finest but homemade by the restaurant's owner, who often doubles as a waiter. **Gradska Vijećnica** (Trg Republike Hrvatske 3, tel. 022/213-605, 9 A.M.–midnight daily, 50Kn) is located on the main square in the old Venetian town hall. It's usually not all that busy, but don't let that scare you away. The food is decent, the prices good, and the location excellent. However, the best table in town has to be at **C Pelegrini** (Jurja Dalmatinca 1, tel. 022/213-701, www.pelegrini.hr, 8 A.M.–midnight daily, 90Kn), set just across from the gorgeous St. Jacob's Cathedral. In good weather you can dine at the few outdoor tables overlooking the water (ideal for a superb breakfast) or in the open-air courtyard just beyond the restaurant (open only at night in season). In the winter dine inside the restaurant's pretty stone-clad space. Anytime of year, the excellent menu, from fried eggs and bacon in the morning to afternoon snacks of olive, cheese, and salted anchovies to mains of roast, risotto, and seafood ravioli, never fails to satisfy.

A 20-minute walk northeast (or take bus #3) from the old town in the suburb of Šubičevac, **Uzorita** (Bana Jelačića 58, tel. 022/213-660, 11 A.M.–1 A.M. daily, 90Kn) has been serving diners since 1898. There's a wonderful terrace surrounded by vines and stone buildings. Fish is the specialty of the house, particularly the mussels.

If you have a car or you're willing to foot the bill for a water taxi (actually a nice way to spend a few minutes), **Zlatna Ribica** (Krapanjskih Spužvara 46, tel. 022/350-695, www.zlatna-ribica.hr, 11 A.M.–11 P.M. daily, 100Kn) in the seaside village of Brodarica, a few kilometers south of Šibenik on the Magistrala (drive, hop a water taxi, or take bus #7), is considered one of the area's finest. The decor is quite average but the fish is always fresh and the view to the tiny island of Krapanj is very nice. The restaurant also rents rooms.

INFORMATION AND SERVICES

The **Šibenik tourist office** (Obala Dr. Franje Tuđmana 5, tel. 022/214-411, www.sibenik-tourism.hr) has some information on the area, though the travel agencies on the Trg Republike Hrvatske, **Atlas** (tel. 022/330-232) and **Cromovens** (tel. 022/212-515, www.cromovens.hr), may be more useful at hooking you up with private rooms and excursions in the region. If you order a drink or snack at **Cafe Castello** (Božidara Petranovića 8, tel. 022/226-385, www.castello.hr), you can at least check your email in the 15 minutes of free Internet access that you get with any purchase.

GETTING THERE AND AROUND

Šibenik's bus station (Draga 14, tel. 060/368-368) is close to the ferry terminal and a short five-minute walk south from the old town. The bus heads frequently to Split (close to two dozen daily, 2 hours, 60Kn), Zadar (close to four dozen a day, 1.5 hours), Dubrovnik (several daily in summer, 6 hours), Rijeka (around a dozen a day in summer, 6 hours), and Zagreb (over a dozen daily in summer, 6.5 hours, 235Kn). Tickets on city buses cost around 10Kn. Bus schedules can be found online at www.atpsi.hr.

Šibenik also has a train station with a couple of daily connections to Zagreb (6.5 hours, 150Kn) and Split (2 hours, 43Kn).

Ferries in town only travel to nearby islands and have no major connections to places like Split.

By car, you can connect with Split (south) or Zadar (north) by simply following the Magistrala or getting back on the highway (a little quicker but less scenic).

AROUND ŠIBENIK
Krka National Park

The Krka National Park (80Kn June–Sept., 65Kn Mar.–May and Oct., 25Kn Jan.–Feb. and Nov.–Dec.) follows the rushing Krka River between Knin and Skradin, the latter of which is located only a 15-minute drive northeast from Šibenik. The entrance at the village of Skradin is where you can pick up boat tours (Mar.–Nov., 70Kn) run by the national park, while at the Lozovac entrance a shuttle bus goes down to the river. Local buses connect Šibenik with Skradin (around 8 connections on weekends, 2 or 3 on weekends, 30 minutes) and the excursion is an easy day trip from Šibenik. Keep in mind that if you want to go further up the river from Visovac to the Krka monastery (additional 70Kn Mar.–Nov.)as described here, you should depart early in the morning—the tour takes around four hours round-trip and schedules make it into a whole-day affair. If you'd like to do the longer tour, it's a good idea to stop by the **Krka National Park office** in Šibenik (Trg Ivana Pavla II 5, tel. 022/217-720, www.npkrka.hr) for more information, or book a package tour through one of the travel agencies in Šibenik.

Boat tours departing from Skradin first stop in the village of Skradinski Buk, where a series of small waterfalls rush over the craggy outcroppings of limestone. One of

ACQUIRING A TASTE FOR *JANJETINA*

Janjetina, or lamb, is a sacred food to many Croatians, particularly those along the coast. Consumed on special occasions and de rigueur at Easter, the best lamb is found in ramshackle roadside establishments on the way to the beach.

Janjetina can be a bit of an acquired taste. In my case, it just seemed sort of, well, fatty, I guess, and not very flavorful. When they served it I felt like I was in a medieval court, with the pieces of meat seemingly hacked off at random and piled on a platter and people digging in without forks or knives.

Word got around about me not being a fan of lamb and suddenly friends and family had made it their mission to introduce me to this food of foods. We were invited to every *roštilj* (cookout) for miles around, with a plate of lamb coming to me first, to see if this would be the one that would succeed in the collective mission to convert me.

Approximately 14 years after I'd first tried *janjetina*, we were spending the week in Šibenik, and after having consumed fish for five days straight my husband mentioned to our friend Mickey that he'd like some *janjetina*. And between Šibenik and Split there is only one real place to go for *janjetina*: Torcida.

Torcida (Donje Polje 42, tel. 022/565-748, www.restoran-torcida.hr, 8 A.M.-11 P.M. daily, 80Kn) is also the name of Split's soccer fan club, so chances were pretty good it would be excellent since Dalmatians do not take anything relating to their soccer lightly.

Torcida is in the middle of nowhere, way up the hill from the coast. Once you think you have certainly passed it and are hopelessly lost, keep going until you see about four dozen cars parked in the arid landscape. Torcida tries to be more than a cinder-block establishment with granite-tile floors. But sophisticated it is not.

Out back is a veritable factory of lamb-on-a-spit, with a dozen spits spinning a dozen lambs. Inside, the tables are packed with families, young and old, most wearing some Italian designer or other, pulling meat off the bones with their teeth, wiping their hands every once in a while on a napkin, taking toothpicks from the handy container in the middle of the table.

The waitress came out to take our order, no menu or pad and pen in sight – because what else would we order anyway? Our table ordered a bottle of white wine, a bottle of mineral water (you mix the two together to make *gemišt*), and lamb.

It was summer and the restaurant was hot. A sign on the front door boasts that it is *klimatazirano* (air-conditioned), but with 500 bodies squished table to table inside, the air-conditioning unit is on the losing end. We refreshed with a couple of glasses of *gemišt* and the waitress came with a basket of bread, a plate of tomatoes and spring onions, and a platter of lamb, still warm from the fire.

Everyone started with forks and knives, but five bites in we were all using fingers to pull and turn and get the sweet meat into our mouths any way possible.

"This is not lamb," I said.

"Ah, but it is," Mickey smiled. "The best lambs are from Dalmatia. And you should see the ones from the islands!"

In Dalmatia, and on islands like Pag, the sheep and lambs feed on little aromatic herbs that grow between the rocks.

"It's like marinating them from birth," Mickey explained.

Whatever it is, that was all I needed to convert. Torcida was what I was looking for. Like my favorite barbecue restaurants back home, it has no pretensions. The decor is nothing special – except, perhaps, for the large framed painting of the Mona Lisa smoking a joint. I faded into a food-induced coma. And I wondered: Just what herbs are those lambs feeding on after all?

the falls spills into a nice pool where you can swim, though you certainly won't be the only one taking a dip. Here you'll also find some peaceful hiking trails through the forests and over the river. From here you can catch the bus to Lozovac or continue further upriver on a boat, visiting the fairy tale–like Franciscan monastery on the tiny island of Visovac, Roški slap, another set of waterfalls, and finally the Krka monastery, a Byzantine-style Serbian Orthodox church and monastery filled with icons and art dating as far back as the 14th century.

You can arrange for private accommodation through Skradin's **tourist office** (Obala bana Šubića 1, tel. 022/771-306, www.skradin.hr) or you can upgrade and stay at the **Hotel Skradinski Buk** (Burinovac bb, tel. 022/771-771, www.skradinskibuk.hr, 540Kn d., including breakfast), where the rooms are on the bland side, but the value for money is better than most hotels in the area. There are several good restaurants around the village of Skradinski Buk. Try the **Konoba Bonaca** (Rokovača 5, tel. 022/771-444, noon–3 p.m. and 5 p.m.–midnight daily, closed Oct.–Apr., 70Kn) or (**Zlatne Školjke** (Grgura Ninskog 9, tel. 022/771-022, www.zlatneskoljke.com, noon–11 p.m. daily, closed mid-Jan.–mid-Feb., 90Kn) for good seafood and local wines.

Krapanj Island

If you're a good swimmer, you could technically swim from the coast in Brodarica (a few kilometers south of Šibenik, take bus #7 or hop a water taxi) and reach the shores of tiny Krapanj Island, just several hundred meters offshore. Its claim to fame is as the smallest inhabited island in Croatia, but it's really known for its sponge diving, the trade that kept it alive for decades. Today sponge diving has largely died out, but the 15th-century **Franjevački samostan** (Franciscan monastery) has a simple **museum** (9 A.M.–noon and 5–7 P.M. Mon.–Sat. June–Sept., 15Kn) following the history of sponge divers on the island. It gets packed in July and August with day-trippers (take a taxi boat from Šibenik or Brodarica), but if you're lucky enough to visit in the off-season it's a sleepy island with its own personality.

Southeast of Šibenik

Thirteen kilometers southeast of Šibenik (take the Magistrala toward Split though you'll soon turn off on the road for Vrpolje) is legendary restaurant (**Torcida** (Donje Polje 42, tel. 022/565-748, www.restoran-torcida.hr, 8 A.M.–11 P.M. daily, 80Kn), famous for its *janjetina*, or spit-roasted lamb. On weekends you'll find it hard to get a table here; it's enormously popular with the local population. It's definitely worth the detour for a taste of true Dalmatia.

Primošten

Once a hopping party town before the Croatian in-crowd moved to Hvar, Primošten has some good restaurants and bars they left behind. The old town is precious, a little island connected by a thin stretch of land to the mainland, and worth a quick walk around before heading out of the now mostly lower-end tourist trade.

SIGHTS

Though there's nothing specific to see in Primošten proper, it's nice to walk around the cobblestone-paved old town before heading up into the hills to the wonderful **Jurlinovi dvori complex** (Draga bb, tel. 022/574-106, info@jurlinovidvori.org, www.jurlinovidvori.org, call to reserve a visit, if you can't get anyone who speaks English have a local tourist office or your hotel call for you) in the preserved village of Draga. Stone houses are clustered around a central courtyard, and each small home is part of the museum, showcasing a traditional Dalmatian kitchen, living room, cellar, sleeping quarters, and a domestic chapel. One home also holds a collection of sacral objects.

Nearby is a 13th-century Romanesque chapel, the church of St. George. The whole place has a laid-back air, preserving history and showing it off to tourists without being gimmicky. It's also one of the few places in Dalmatia where you can get a look at the history and culture of the people.

WINERIES

Wine lovers and foodies will find a couple of gems in town. The local Babić wine has a specific salty taste, certainly worth a try, and lobster prepared in the local style is a must-try at one of the better restaurants in town. Check with the tourist office for excursions and tours of the local wine trails, through the rocky villages of Burnji in the hills above Primošten.

BEACHES

There's a big beach fronting the cafés and tacky souvenir shops along the street connecting the parking lot and the old town. It's usually quite crowded, though the convenience to a coffee is not bad. Better beaches can be found by walking along the promenade to the north of town.

ACCOMMODATIONS AND FOOD

Book private rooms from **Agency Nik** (Trg Stjepana Radića 1, tel. 022/571-200, www.nik.hr). Another option is the Tito-era package hotel **Zora** (Raduča bb, tel. 022/581-022, www.azaleahotels.com, 1,060Kn d., including breakfast), with an ugly unpromising exterior but clean, basic rooms a 10-minute scenic walk to the old town. Guests rave about the idyllic location, which must make up for the lack of character and updates to the property. However, the price in-season makes private accommodation a better bet.

An absolute must-eat is the charming step-back-in-time **Jurlinovi dvori** (Draga bb, tel. 022/574-106, info@jurlinovidvori.org, www.jurlinovidvori.org, call to arrange a meal, if you can't get anyone who speaks English have a local tourist office or your hotel call for you), with excellent local cuisine, warm hospitality, and a one-of-a-kind experience in the hills above Primošten. Back in town you'll find lots of *konoba*-style restaurants and pizzerias. For a really great view and filling food, try **Restoran Babilon** (Težačka 15, tel. 022/570-769, noon–2 P.M. and 6–8 P.M., closed Oct.–Apr., 85Kn) and its charming open-air dining.

GETTING THERE AND AROUND

Take buses #14, #15, or #16 from Šibenik during weekdays (on weekends take the #16, at least once daily, 30 minutes) to get to Primošten. If you're driving, it's about 20 kilometers south of Šibenik. You'll exit right off the Magistrala (well, it's more of a turn than an exit). Once you're in town there are at least two small lots where you can pay to park (around 10Kn an hour in summer). From the lot, walk south along the waterfront to reach the old town area.

Trogir

A postcard-perfect prosperous fishing village with a lively Riva for strolling after dark, Trogir also has some charming architecture. Beaches are just across the bridge on the island of Čiovo, though the best ones are found by boat, on some of the almost uninhabited islands offshore. Trogir fills up in the height of summer, making it hard to walk, let alone enjoy the full beauty of the place. Its proximity to Split and Split's airport however, make it a worthwhile stopping-off point if you're in transit.

SIGHTS
Kopnena vrata
Land Gate

When you enter Trogir, passing the little market on the right and crossing the small bridge, you'll see the big 17th-century Kopnena vrata. The guy on the top is the town's Sveti Ivan (St. John), a local 12th-century bishop locals claim was blessed with miracle-working powers. Following the road leading through the gate, you'll arrive at the **Gradski muzej** (Town Museum, Gradska vrata 4, tel. 021/881-406, Mon.–Sat. 9 A.M.–1 P.M. and 5–10 P.M. July–Aug., 9 A.M.–noon and 5–8 P.M. June–Sept., 9 A.M.–2 P.M. Oct.–May, 10Kn). Inside is a small display of photographs, documents, local costumes, and a few pieces of artwork and archaeology. It's only a small view of Trogir's past, though the courtyard is charming and the museum sometimes has *klapa* concerts during the summer, making it a worthwhile stop.

Katedrala svetog Lovrijenca
St. Lawrence's Cathedral

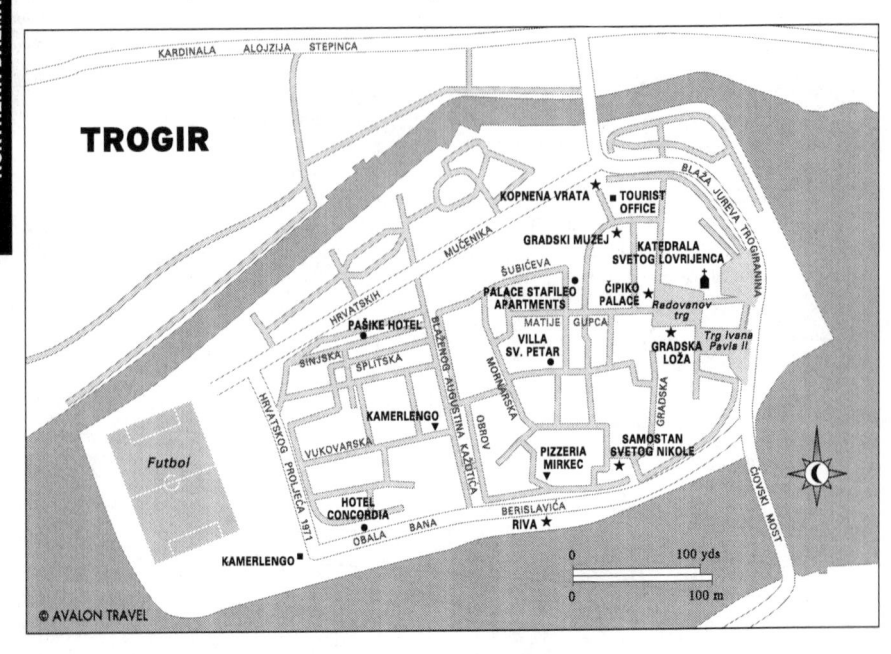

On Trg Ivana Pavla II, arguably Trogir's nicest square, are the must-see early 13th-century (though it wasn't completely finished until the 15th century) Katedrala svetog Lovrijenca (tel. 021/881-426, 9 A.M.–7 P.M. Mon.–Sat. and mass on Sun., 9 A.M.–noon in winter, hours are not always observed, free) and its much later addition, the Venetian bell tower seen peeking above Trogir's red tiled roofs. If the tower's open you can climb the almost 50 meters to the top for about 10Kn and get some nice views of Trogir. The most stunning feature of the church is the western portal, where wonderful reliefs by the 13th-century stone carver Radovan compete for attention in a busy amalgam of reality and fantasy. The interior of the church depicts scenes from the life of Sveti Ivan of Trogir. Opening off the north of the interior, the **Kapela svetog Ivana Trogirskog** (St. John of Trogir's Chapel) has an impressive ceiling populated by angels carved by apprentices of the renowned Dalmatinac. Beyond the chapel you'll find a small *riznica* (treasury, 9 A.M.–7 P.M. Mon.–Sat., 10Kn) with a smattering of gilt and carvings.

Čipiko Palace

Just across from the cathedral on Trg Ivana Pavla II is the Čipiko Palace, a decaying Venetian-style home that's pretty to admire from the outside, but with nothing to see on the inside. It's significant to the city since it was home of the Čipiko family, a family of nobles important to Trogir in the Renaissance. The family dabbled in seafaring military life and literary pursuits, as well as funding some of the cathedral's stash of art and sculpture.

Gradska loža
Town Loggia

You'll also find the Gradska loža on the Trg Ivana Pavla II. Though the loggia was restored in the late 1800s, many of its ornate reliefs date back to the Middle Ages. The one that doesn't was actually carved by Meštrović, of the Bishop Petar Berislavić, on the loggia's south wall. Next door in a former bishop's palace is the **Pinakoteka** (tel. 021/881-426, 9 A.M.–8 P.M. Mon.–Sat. and 3–7 P.M. Sun. June–Sept., call for winter hours, 20Kn), which houses an attractive collection of Trogir's sacral art, including a 15th-century altarpiece by local painter Blaž Jurjev of the Madonna and Child with the saints.

Čiovo Island, with beaches just across the bridge from Trogir's old town

FINDING YOUR OWN PRIVATE PARADISE

If you really want to find a stretch of deserted beach, it's not that hard to do in Croatia, with hundreds of uninhabited islands just off the coast. The first thing to do is to ask the locals, though keep in mind that another person's idea of paradise may be very different from your own. If you're used to navigating a boat, rent one from the marina and set out to find your own spot, either mooring offshore or parking one of those inflatable types right on the beach. Not confident with taking to the high seas? Rent a water taxi with a captain who can take you there, perhaps even negotiating a fish picnic in the deal. Of course, you'll see lots of advertisements for these fish picnics, but unless you want to share them with 20 other hungry tourists, it's better to hire your own private boat. If all else fails, walk. Usually just beyond the beach where everyone is packed in is a beach where everyone isn't. It's probably harder to get to, just short of requiring rock-climbing skills (at least remember to wear a pair of thick-soled shoes), but you're usually rewarded for your efforts.

Because a private beach usually means a remote one, make sure you don't go so far that you get lost, and bring plenty of supplies, because if you're hungry or thirsty, even paradise doesn't seem so great.

Finding a private beach is not that hard to do in Croatia.

Samostan svetog Nikole
Convent of St. Nicholas

South of Trg Ivana Pavla II, the Samostan svetog Nikole (tel. 021/881-631, 10 A.M.–noon and 4–6:30 P.M. in summer, contact tourist office for out-of-season hours, 15Kn) is worth the trip for its Greek relief of Kairos from the 3rd century and for its treasure-chest haul of icons and art from the 13th to 17th centuries. Most touching are the hope chests carried by young girls entering the convent.

Riva

Following along the water is the wide café-and-yacht-lined Riva, which fills with tourists and locals on summer evenings. At the far end you'll see the 15th-century **Kamerlengo** (9 A.M.–7 P.M. daily in summer, 10Kn), a medieval fortress that has nice views from the top and hosts open-air movies and concerts during the hottest months.

BEACHES

The best beaches directly around Trogir are on **Čiovo Island,** just across the bridge from the old town. Turning to the left after the bridge you'll see a few convenient, but usually crowded, beaches. The best are found by driving until the road turns to gravel and continuing further (all the way until the old quarry if you like) and finding a stretch of beach backed by a few trees for some quiet lounging. If you see a couple of kids charging an entrance fee, feel free to hand them a few kuna. If you don't have a car, hire a boat and captain for the day (try friendly local Mario Oštrić at tel. 095/806-0382 or 091/530-1802) to take you on a private fish picnic to one of the uninhabited, or barely inhabited, islands offshore. Looking for something a bit longer or luxurious? Mario's dad is the cook on the **Gullet Andi** (tel. 091/188-7136, ante.slamic@st.t-com.hr, www.gulets-andi.com, contact for prices and schedules), a beautiful wooden sailboat shuttling passengers on seven-day cruises around the Dalmatian islands, departing from Trogir.

ENTERTAINMENT AND EVENTS

Though Trogir's not really a party town, there's a decent selection of spots to drink and dance. Quieter sorts should try the bars in **Radovanov trg,** the square behind the cathedral. Those looking for something louder should hit the cafés along the Riva, often hosting live bands in the summer, or the local favorite **Martinino** (Hrvatskih Mučenika 2, no phone, 8 A.M.–1 A.M. daily) near the Land Gate.

In summer the city of Trogir plays host to a number of music groups, from pop to classical to folk, during its **Trogirsko kulturno ljeto** (Trogir Cultural Summer, July–Aug.). Check with the tourist office to see what's playing.

ACCOMMODATIONS

If you plan on roughing it, **Camp Seget** (Hrvatskih žrtava 121, tel. 021/880-394, www.kamp-seget.hr, 120Kn) is located two kilometers north from Trogir. The camp has space for tents and RVs plus a handful of hostel-type rooms. For private rooms, try **Travel Agency Portal** (Obala bana Berislavića 3, tel. 021/885-016, www.portal-trogir.com), with a decent selection of old town accommodation as well as beachfront rooms, apartments, and villas. It's advisable to book ahead for the best spots.

The **Palace Domus Maritima** (Put Cumbrijana 10, tel. 091/513-7802, www.domus-maritima.com, 604Kn d.) is located in a 400-year-old stone building just across the bridge from the old town on the island of Čiovo,

making it about a three-minute walk into town. The hotel has a rough-around-the-edges elegance. The comfortably furnished rooms have exposed stone walls and slightly garish (and often nude) original art serving as decor. There is a decent restaurant on the premises and you can arrange for art workshops in advance. The best thing about the **Hotel Concordia** (Obala Bana Berislavića 22, tel. 021/885-400, www.concordia-hotel.net, 680Kn d., including breakfast) is its location, right on the harborfront promenade of old Trogir. The position on the Riva, which pulses with thousands of tourists on summer nights, makes it convenient but certainly not the quietest location in town. The furnishings in the small rooms are very plain, though their 1960s vibe almost makes them swank, and the hotel can help arrange free parking nearby.

The **Pašike Hotel** (Sinjska bb, tel. 021/885-185, www.hotelpasike.com, 800Kn d., including breakfast) is located down a narrow little street in Trogir's medieval core, furnished with wonderful antiques in a bit of an organic fashion.

The **Palace Stafileo apartments** (Budislavićeva 6, tel. 091/731-7607, www.trogironline.com/stafileo, 426Kn d.) offers excellent value for money. The rooms in the 15th-century center-of-town palace don't have a lot of character, but they have satellite television, air-conditioning, and small kitchens.

Villa Sv. Petar (Ivana Duknovica 14, tel. 021/884-359, www.villa-svpetar.com, 820Kn d.) is another convenient option set in a stone building in the heart of the old town. The furnishings are fairly simple but the service is great. Ask for a room with exposed stone walls for the most authentic charm.

FOOD

For a casual meal, try **Pizzeria Mirkec** (Budislavićeva 15, tel. 021/883-042, open 11 A.M.–midnight daily in summer, call for off-season hours, 60Kn) for good pizzas and pasta dishes, served outside on the bustling Riva-front (with a great show of people-watching during dinner) in the summer or inside the tiny upstairs dining room in winter. **Škrapa** (Hrvatskih Mučenika 9, tel. 021/885-313, noon–11 P.M. daily in summer, noon–11 P.M. Mon.–Sat. in winter, 65Kn) has a good selection of simple local dishes at friendly prices. You can dine indoors or out at the cozy little *konoba*. **Kamerlengo** (Vukovarska 2, tel. 021/884-772, www.kamerlengo.hr, 9 A.M.–midnight daily, 90Kn) is a reliable choice for grilled fish in the center of the old town, though the most interesting place to eat in town is probably **Čelica** (otok Čiovo-Lučica, tel. 021/882-3440, 11 A.M.–midnight daily in summer, 4–11 P.M. daily in winter, no credit cards, 85Kn), located on a defunct wooden car ferry just across the little bridge on the island of Čiovo. It's not overpriced and the dishes, mostly seafood, are good quality.

INFORMATION AND SERVICES

Trogir's **tourist office** (Ivana Pavla II broj 1, tel. 021/881-412, 8 A.M.–9 P.M. daily June–Sept., 8 A.M.–2 P.M. Mon.–Fri. Oct.–May) can provide maps, brochures, and information on private accommodation. The bus station has a left-luggage office (9 A.M.–10 P.M. daily, 15Kn a day).

GETTING THERE AND AROUND

It's easy to get to Trogir from Split's airport. Take bus #37, which runs every 20 minutes and takes about 20 minutes. Trogir's small bus station (tel. 021/881-405), across from the market, has multiple connections with Split daily (buses leave every 20 minutes, about 1.5 hours due to all the stops). There's also a ferry for Split, which takes an hour and runs four times a day in the summer. Check with the tourist office for more information on schedules. It's easy to walk around Trogir's main town and possible but a bit risky (due to traffic) to stroll to some of the first beaches on Čiovo Island. To get to the best beaches you'll need to have a car or hire a boat.

AROUND TROGIR
Kaštela

Hugging the shoreline between Trogir and Split is a series of villages referred to as Kaštela. There's some pretty architecture here as each village is formed around a castle built centuries ago to protect crops and property. Today the villages are decidedly more local than most towns on the Dalmatian coast, even in the height of summer. The prettiest village is **Kaštel Gomilica**, though **Kaštel Kambelovac** has a good, reasonable restaurant in the **Baletna Škola** (Ante Starčevića, tel. 021/220-208, 8 A.M.–midnight daily, 80Kn), located in a former ballet school that looks more like a rustic fisherman's house. The villages are great for walking from bar to bar in the evenings along the waterfront promenade starting in **Kaštel Štafilić** and ending in **Kaštel Stari**. Bus #37 to Split makes stops at each village.

Drvenik Mali and Drvenik Veli

A daily morning ferry connects Trogir with Drvenik Veli and Drvenik Mali Islands (connections tend to be in the early morning and then evening since the ferry services people who live on the islands but work in Trogir). The best beach is on Drvenik Veli at **Krknjaši Bay,** a stretch of pebbly beach and clear water backed by a simple seafood restaurant of outstandingly high quality, **Krknjaši** (Uvala Krknjaši, tel. 021/893-073, 11 A.M.–11 P.M. in summer, 70Kn), open only in the summer. The family's fish soup is highly recommended.

The beach is about a 45-minute walk from the ferry stop, though, so give yourself time to make the boat's early-evening departure, around 6 P.M. Drvenik Veli is also a nice place to hike through the rural roads and olive trees. Drvenik Mali is the smaller and wilder of the two islands, with some excellent beaches (the sandy one at **Vela Rina** is likely the best), though you won't find any restaurants or cafés nor much in the way of shade, so pack a picnic and a small umbrella.

www.moon.com

DESTINATIONS | ACTIVITIES | BLOGS | MAPS | BOOKS

MOON.COM is all new, and ready to help plan your next trip! Filled with fresh trip ideas and strategies, author interviews, informative blogs, a detailed map library, and descriptions of all the Moon guidebooks, Moon.com is all you need to get out and explore the world—or even places in your own backyard. As always, when you travel with Moon, expect an experience that is uncommon and truly unique.

MAP SYMBOLS

	Expressway	◖	Highlight	✗	Airfield	⚓	Golf Course
	Primary Road	○	City/Town	✈	Airport	🅿	Parking Area
	Secondary Road	◉	State Capital	▲	Mountain	⏶	Archaeological Site
	Unpaved Road	✺	National Capital	✦	Unique Natural Feature	⛪	Church
	Trail	★	Point of Interest			⛽	Gas Station
	Ferry	•	Accommodation		Waterfall		Glacier
	Railroad	▼	Restaurant/Bar	▲	Park		Mangrove
	Pedestrian Walkway	■	Other Location	⛉	Trailhead		Reef
	Stairs	△	Campground	⛷	Skiing Area		Swamp

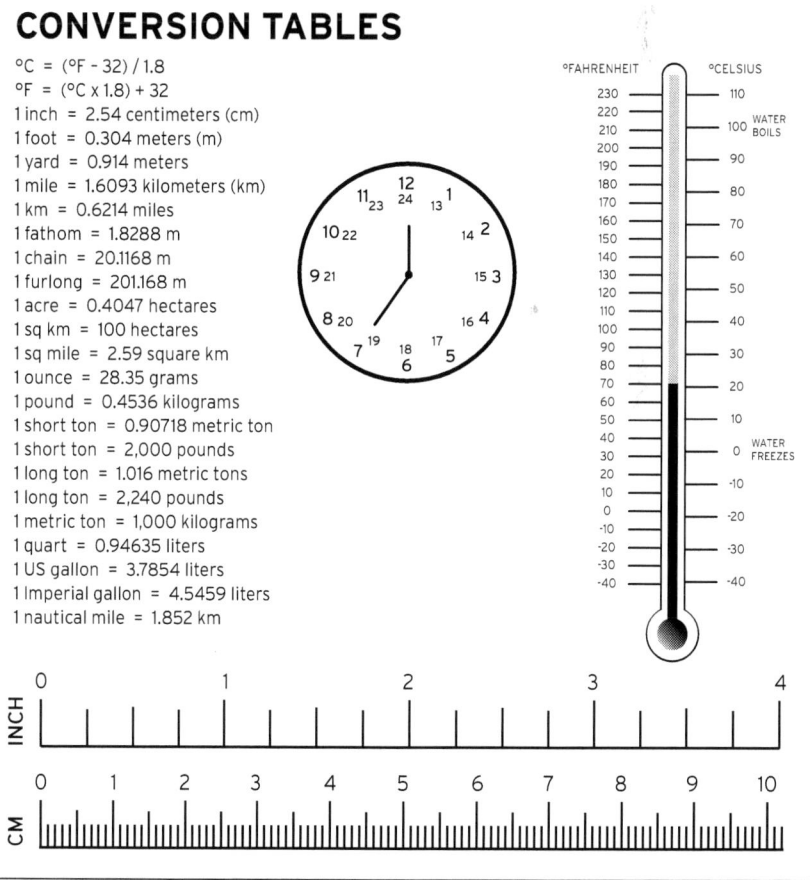

CONVERSION TABLES

°C = (°F − 32) / 1.8
°F = (°C x 1.8) + 32
1 inch = 2.54 centimeters (cm)
1 foot = 0.304 meters (m)
1 yard = 0.914 meters
1 mile = 1.6093 kilometers (km)
1 km = 0.6214 miles
1 fathom = 1.8288 m
1 chain = 20.1168 m
1 furlong = 201.168 m
1 acre = 0.4047 hectares
1 sq km = 100 hectares
1 sq mile = 2.59 square km
1 ounce = 28.35 grams
1 pound = 0.4536 kilograms
1 short ton = 0.90718 metric ton
1 short ton = 2,000 pounds
1 long ton = 1.016 metric tons
1 long ton = 2,240 pounds
1 metric ton = 1,000 kilograms
1 quart = 0.94635 liters
1 US gallon = 3.7854 liters
1 Imperial gallon = 4.5459 liters
1 nautical mile = 1.852 km

°FAHRENHEIT	°CELSIUS	
230	110	
220	100	WATER BOILS
210		
200	90	
190	80	
180		
170	70	
160		
150	60	
140		
130	50	
120		
110	40	
100		
90	30	
80		
70	20	
60		
50	10	
40		
30	0	WATER FREEZES
20		
10	−10	
0		
−10	−20	
−20	−30	
−30		
−40	−40	

MOON DUBROVNIK &
THE DALMATION COAST
Avalon Travel
a member of the Perseus Books Group
1700 Fourth Street
Berkeley, CA 94710, USA
www.moon.com

Editor and Series Manager: Kathryn Ettinger
Copy Editor: Amy Scott
Graphics Coordinator: Kathryn Osgood
Production Coordinator: Darren Alessi
Cover Designer: Kathryn Osgood
Map Editor: Brice Ticen
Cartographers: Kat Bennett, Chris Markiewicz
Proofreader: Julie Littman

ISBN-13: 978-1-59880-543-7

Text © 2009 by Shann Fountain Čulo.
Maps © 2009 by Avalon Travel.
All rights reserved.

Some photos and illustrations are used by permission and are the property of the original copyright owners.

Front cover photo: View of Rovinj, Croatia, from the water © istockphoto.com
Title page photo: Dubrovnik view © Florian Siebeck/ commons.wikimedia.org

Printed in the United States

Moon Spotlight and the Moon logo are the property of Avalon Travel. All other marks and logos depicted are the property of the original owners. All rights reserved. No part of this book may be translated or reproduced in any form, except brief extracts by a reviewer for the purpose of a review, without written permission of the copyright owner.

Although every effort was made to ensure that the information was correct at the time of going to press, the author and publisher do not assume and hereby disclaim any liability to any party for any loss or damage caused by errors, omissions, or any potential travel disruption due to labor or financial difficulty, whether such errors or omissions result from negligence, accident, or any other cause.

ABOUT THE AUTHOR

Shann Fountain Čulo

Born in South Carolina, Shann Fountain Čulo has been traveling all of her life. She studied abroad in both Spain and Germany and has visited 26 countries – many of them before age 21. She speaks Spanish, Croatian, and rapidly declining French.

After graduating from Sweet Briar College, Shann owned a multilingual staffing company, tried her hand at corporate gifts, and taught Spanish (with occasional travel sabbaticals in between) before becoming a writer. Now a full-time freelance writer, she is a frequent contributor to *Travel + Leisure* and *Condé Nast Traveler*, and her articles have also appeared in *Hemispheres, Four Seasons Hotels Magazine*, and several other publications.

Shann began visiting Eastern Europe in 1992, immediately falling in love with Croatia – and a tall Croatian as well. She made 16 Croatia trips in all, many of them for months at a time, until finally moving there in 2004. She lives in Zagreb, Croatia, with her husband (the tall Croatian) and their two young children. Writing this book, she fell in love with the region all over again, and became a wine connoisseur and an expert in traveling with kids. Shann spends her time writing, gardening, hiking, drinking coffee, and standing in line. That's Rule #4 of living in Croatia: Get used to bureaucracy.